9.75

D0915417

BRITISH MEMBERS OF PARLIAMENT

Also by Anthony King

THE BRITISH GENERAL ELECTION OF 1964
(with David Butler)

THE BRITISH GENERAL ELECTION OF 1966
(with David Butler)

THE BRITISH PRIME MINISTER *(editor)*

WESTMINSTER AND BEYOND   *(with Anne Sloman)*

British Members of Parliament: A Self-Portrait

ANTHONY KING
University of Essex

With a Foreword by
BRIAN LAPPING AND NORMA PERCY
'State of the Nation', Granada Television

M

In association with
Granada Television

First published 1974 by
THE MACMILLAN PRESS LTD
London and Basingstoke
Associated companies in New York
Dublin Melbourne Johannesburg and Madras

SBN 333 17170 5

Typeset by
COMPUTATYPE (UK) LTD
Fort William

Printed in Great Britain by
LEWIS REPRINTS LTD
London and Tonbridge

Contents

Foreword

This book is a by-product of a television programme, *The State of the Nation: Parliament*, made by Granada Television and transmitted on the British independent television network over three evenings in July 1973. The production team began its work with an unusual instruction: 'Spend as long as you need to find out what people really in the know think is wrong with Parliament and how they think it can be put right. And don't worry about the form of the programme until the research process is completed.'

We began with the thesis that people are dissatisfied with Parliament and, to prove it, we commissioned the biggest survey yet undertaken of public attitudes to Parliament. At the same time, we explored one way to improve the MP's ability to satisfy his electorate: by strengthening his constituency 'surgery' with permanent staff and a shop on his local high street. But the results of the survey (a full analysis by Ivor Crewe of the University of Essex is to be published by Macmillan shortly) showed that a majority of the public expressed a consistently high level of satisfaction with Parliament and their own MP. This result shook us. If the people were satisfied with Parliament, why produce programmes advocating its reform? The answer was that our talks with MPs, civil servants and journalists had convinced us there was considerable dissatisfaction among those most closely involved.

What did the participants themselves think was wrong? This book results from our main effort to find out. During a trip to Washington, Norma Percy met John Brademas, a Democratic whip in the House of Representatives, who kept replying to her questions about a Congressman's work by saying, 'That's in the Brookings Institution book by Charles Clapp.' The Brookings method of tape-recording, transcribing and editing dinner conversations was adapted by us — as Anthony King describes in Chapter 1 — both to produce this book and to sift through the ideas discovered in our year's research.

We lost no time asking Anthony King to perform the dual

role of chairman at the dinners and author of this book. His co-authorship of two of the Nuffield general election studies, his conduct of the perceptive BBC radio series, *Talking Politics*, and the fact that anyone studying British politics keeps bumping into his writings, all made him the obvious choice. And, when we put it to him, we discovered another reason: he seemed to be the only person in England who had read both Charles Clapp's book and the previous Brookings dinners book, by Marver Bernstein, about the work of American civil servants.

The dinners taught us a number of lessons. First, our belief in the frustration, sometimes bordering on a sense of futility, of the back-bench MP was confirmed. It is often supposed (see particularly Chapters 7 and 9) that this frustration comes from the repressive discipline of the whips. It doesn't. The MPs at the dinners made it clear (Chapter 5) that the whips seldom try to change the vote of a rebellious backbencher and haven't much power if they do try. The frustration centres around the MP's attempts to influence those inside the government machine, ministers and civil servants, through existing parliamentary processes, often after the real decisions have been taken (Chapters 7 and 9). The present standing committee system for scrutiny of legislation was particularly criticised. On the other hand, most of the MPs at the dinners valued investigatory select committees, which question ministers, civil servants and experts (Chapter 8), though they disagreed about whether an extension or strengthening of these committees was the way to increase Parliament's effectiveness.

These points became the central themes in our programme.* The first part showed what happened behind the public façade as two clauses of the Fair Trading Bill went through the Commons Standing Committee: the result of four months' filming of civil servants and ministers in the Department of Trade and Industry, as well as of MPs in parts of the House of Commons. In the second part, a group of MPs held a select committee-type inquiry on whether Parliament had lost control of the government machine; and in the final part MPs

* The transcript of the programme with an extended description of the thinking behind it was published by Granada Television in October 1973.

debated whether an extension of investigatory select committees was the best way to inform MPs of government activity and increase Parliament's influence. The programme, like this book, tried to show how Parliament really works and to give the MPs themselves a platform to discuss reform.

B.L.
N.P.

Acknowledgements

This book is mainly the work of the Members of Parliament who took part in the discussion dinners described in Chapter 1. My role was simply to prepare agendas for the dinners, to chair them, and to write up the results afterwards. I am grateful to all the MPs for their patience and good humour at the time and for taking the trouble to read and comment on the typescript of this book. I am especially grateful to Granada Television for sponsoring the dinners, and to Brian Lapping and Norma Percy of Granada, who originally had the idea of holding the dinners, who made all of the detailed arrangements for them, and who also made dozens of suggestions — almost all of which I accepted — for improving the chapters that follow. Typing the transcripts of the dinners was a prodigious job; it was done astonishingly quickly and remarkably accurately by Roz Hair, who also helped organise the sound recording at the dinners, and Sally Askey. My own secretary at the University of Essex, June Palmer, typed the final manuscript. I greatly appreciate the help of all of them. It goes without saying that for the book as it now stands I bear sole responsibility.

A. K.

1 December 1973

1 The Granada Dinners

Late in 1972 nineteen Members of Parliament – nine Conservative and ten Labour – took part in a series of discussion dinners organised by Granada Television. The dinners were held in a private dining-room in the United Oxford and Cambridge University Club in London, some five minutes' drive from the House of Commons. They started early in the evening and went on until about 10 o'clock depending on whether or not there was a vote in the House that night. There were eight dinners altogether; at four only Labour MPs were present, at the other four only Conservatives. Each Member was invited to all four dinners for his party, but of course not everyone was able to attend every time; two Members had to miss two of the dinners, another twelve each missed one. The discussions at the dinners were tape-recorded and transcribed. The resulting verbatim record amounts to some 170,000 words and forms the basis of this book.

The main reason for holding the dinners was quite straightforward. A large number of academic books and articles on the House of Commons is published every year, and Parliament is extensively covered on television and in the press. Yet, so far as we know, there has never appeared in print an extended description of the work of Members of Parliament as they themselves experience it. What is life like if you are an MP? How do you spend your time? What do you do for your constituents? How do you keep your supporters happy? What is your relationship with the whips? How do you set about trying to influence the Government? And so on. These were the sort of questions discussed at the dinners. We asked the Members who attended to talk as far as possible not in generalities but in concrete detail and in terms of their own experiences. The aim was to produce an account that would convey to the reader a vivid sense of what the MP's job is really like – and of what are some of the great issues facing the modern House of Commons.

Our Members were not a random sample of all MPs. First,

for obvious reasons the organisers of the dinners wanted to
avoid inviting Members who would talk too much – or too
little. An effort was also made to avoid obstreperous Members
and pairs of Members known to dislike each other. Second,
members of the Government and the Opposition shadow cabinet were ruled out, partly because it was assumed that they
would be too busy to come, but mainly because the focus of
the dinners was meant to be on the backbencher. Indeed one
of the things we wanted to explore was precisely the relationship between backbenchers – the great majority of the
House – and their own leaders. Even so, seven of our nineteen
Members had served in Government at some time in the past,
and two were currently Opposition spokesmen although not
members of the shadow cabinet. No whips were invited because it was thought their presence would be inhibiting.

Otherwise an effort was made to invite a broadly representative group. Four of the nineteen were first elected in 1970,
another four in or before 1959. The geographical spread was
not perfect – we had no one representing a Welsh or an East
Anglian constituency – but three of our nineteen were Scots,
and most other parts of the country were covered. Marginal
and safe seats were represented, and so were rural and semi-
rural. No particular effort was made to invite a woman because it was thought (rightly or wrongly) that a woman's experiences in Parliament would not differ significantly from a
man's.

Politically, the nineteen reflected all shades of opinion in the
two parties. At the Labour dinners there was something of an
over-weighting – wholly unintended – in favour of pro-Com-
mon Market MPs; no fewer than five of the ten Labour Members had voted with the Government in favour of joining the
EEC in the crucial division in October 1971. But the Labour
contingent also included two prominent members of the Tribune Group, and two of the ten were trade-union sponsored.
The Conservatives included several Members on the liberal
wing of the party, one whole-hearted admirer of Enoch Powell, and two anti-Common Market rebels. Taken as a group,
the nineteen were somewhat younger on average than the
House as a whole and – probably most Members would
agree – more able and articulate.

The nineteen were:

Conservative
Sydney Chapman (Birmingham, Handsworth)
David Crouch (Canterbury)
Rt. Hon. William Deedes (Ashford)
Philip Goodhart (Beckenham)
David Knox (Leek)
Michael McNair-Wilson (Walthamstow East)
Neil Marten (Banbury)
Nicholas Scott (Paddington South)
Edward Taylor (Glasgow, Cathcart)

Labour
Norman Atkinson (Tottenham)
Michael Barnes (Brentford and Chiswick)
Norman Buchan (Renfrewshire West)
George Cunningham (Islington South-West)
Rt. Hon. Edmund Dell (Birkenhead)
Dickson Mabon (Greenock)
Michael Meacher (Oldham West)
William Price (Rugby)
Ivor Richard (Barons Court)
James Tinn (Cleveland).

The Members of the two parties were invited to meet separately in the belief that they would talk more freely alone than in the presence of their opponents. They were promised that nothing would be attributed to them directly and that any statement that could embarrass them would not be reproduced in such a way that it could be traced to them. The dinners, in other words, were held on strict 'lobby terms'. In consequence, the conversation was remarkably uninhibited and relaxed; the MPs did not seem shy either of each other or of the microphones. But the reader should be warned that, in order to keep our promise, we have had to edit fairly drastically some of the passages below. The sense of each passage has been retained, but references to particular individuals, constituencies, incidents and so on have often been altered or deleted. Indeed, in several cases passages that might be thought embarrassing to particular Members have had false clues added to them. The reader should also be warned that of course conversation over dinner is a less precise form of communication than the written word; not the least of the reasons for maintaining anonymity is that selections from the transcripts of an oral discussion may — however fair the selector tries to be — give a misleading impression of a speaker's views.

The differences between the Conservative and Labour dinners were striking. The typical Conservative dinner was pleasant and relaxed, but at the same time highly business-like. The agenda, circulated beforehand, was adhered to fairly closely and Members tended to apologise if they strayed from it. Much of what they said could have been said by members of either party and, although the Conservatives disagreed with one another quite often, they usually did so only when it was apparent that their disagreement was directly relevant to the purposes of the book. They were not disposed to interrupt one another and, when the discussion got too lively for the microphones, were prepared to give way to the chairman.

The Labour dinners were altogether more boisterous. The Labour Members clearly enjoyed the sport of talking and arguing for its own sake, and it usually took half as long again to cover any given item on the agenda. Anyone who started a hare — however unrelated to whatever was currently being discussed — could be sure that it would be chased all over the field, and sometimes into neighbouring fields. The discussion at the Labour dinners was highly political and was much more likely than that at the Tory dinners to move from descriptions of the world as it now is to considerations of the world as it ought to be. Above all, the Labour MPs emerged as individualists, each determined that his own views should not be confused with anybody else's. The Conservatives reminded one of a well-disciplined rugby team, with the considerable talents of each individual player put at the disposal of the side as a whole. The Labour MPs, by contrast, resembled a troupe of travelling tennis professionals, every member anxious to pit his own talents against those of all the others. There were individual exceptions on both sides, of course; but they were exceptions. All the same, the level of discussion at both series of dinners was extraordinarily high, and MPs of both parties have contributed equally to the chapters that follow.

The Granada dinners were modelled fairly closely on a similar series of dinners organised in the late 1950s by the Brookings Institution of Washington in the United States. All of the MPs who attended the Granada dinners were given a copy of the book that resulted from the earlier dinners: *The Congressman: His Work as He Sees It,* Charles L. Clapp (Brookings, Washington, D.C., 1963). Two differences between the British and the American exercises are worth noting. The first is that, although it is impossible to be sure without seeing the full transcripts of the Brookings dinners, the British MPs seem to have talked more freely and incisively than the American congressmen; the views of the American congressmen seem more conventional. The second is that unfortunately the British dinners were a more limited affair than the American. Whereas nineteen MPs participated in the British dinners, nearly twice that number, thirty-six, took part in the American; and, whereas altogether eight dinners were held in London, again twice that number, sixteen, were held in Washington. The result is that, whatever the relative strengths and weaknesses of the contributions on the two sides of the Atlantic, the Brookings volume is based on far more material than this one.

The reader should bear in mind throughout the limitations of the discussion method. Our dinners were held in the late months of 1972, when the Conservative Government was unpopular with many of its own back-bench supporters and when the Labour Party was badly divided, particularly on Europe. It may be that in subtle ways what was said at the dinners would have been different if they had been held (say) a year earlier or a year later; it would obviously also have made a great difference if a Labour rather than a Conservative Government had been in power. The reader should bear in mind, too, that the experiences and views set out below are those of the nineteen MPs who happened to participate. It is hardly likely that another nineteen would have said exactly the same things. With these qualifications, however, we believe that the portrait of parliamentary life that emerges below does not relate only to late 1972 and would be accepted as broadly accurate by the great majority of Members of Parliament.

One last cautionary word to anyone who might suppose that he will find here a single, definitive account of 'the work of an

MP'. What struck everyone at the dinners was the variety in what was said: not merely variety in opinions and value-judgements, but variety in the ways MPs spend their time, variety in the ways they organise such simple things as their constituency surgeries, variety in their responses to common political problems. Members of Parliament do have much in common, and a more systematic piece of research than this would probably have brought some degree of analytic order out of the present seeming chaos. In what follows, however, our nineteen MPs have largely been left to speak for themselves, and it is a sense of variety, and often of inconclusiveness, that is conveyed. There are, after all, as many ways of being an MP as there are MPs. No attempt has been made in the following pages to conceal this fact.

2 The Constituency Party

Every Member of Parliament is involved in an almost endless series of relationships: with those who voted for him and with those who did not, with colleagues in the House of Commons, with outside interest groups, with ministers and so on. But perhaps an MP's primary relationship – the one that takes precedence – is with his local Labour party or Conservative association. As one of our Members put it:

I don't think there is a single Member of Parliament who, unless he's already announced that he's going to retire at the next election, can afford to regard his local people with contempt. All of us in our varying ways pay attention to them.

Very few of the disagreements that develop between Members and their supporters find their way into the national newspapers; but there are innumerable potential sources of conflict – over how much time the MP spends in his constituency, over his handling of particular constituency problems, over important matters of national policy – and no less than nine of our nineteen MPs admitted to having been in some difficulty with their local party at one time or another.

In most cases the trouble did not amount to much. One Labour Member had publicly supported the Labour Government's cuts in public expenditure in 1968 and had then in 1971 refused to support the party line on the Common Market.

In the first case I was got out of trouble by the precipitate action of my left-wingers, who attacked the cuts seeing this as an opportunity to get at me. They rushed into the local press with a letter condemning me – with the result that overnight there was a tremendous swing in the party behind me. Over the Common Market I was subject to constituency pressure and union pressure [this MP is a sponsored trade-union Member]. But no consequences flowed from my going against both. In fact I heard afterwards – not at the time – that my union executive had taken a specific decision that, while they were to use all sorts of arguments on me, there were to be no consequences if I went against them, as I eventually did. The main pressure I felt was a moral one, because so many of the friends who had stood by me when things were rough under the Labour Government were opposed to me on this, and I felt really sad about having to go against them.

A Conservative with a semi-rural constituency had also experienced some difficulty over the Common Market — 'because I'm a strong pro-European'.

I have been in trouble and I've suffered two resignations of very senior officers in the Association because of it — resignations which were publicised in banner headlines across the whole of the front page of the local paper. The chairman of one of my major branches resigned, and one of the principal local councillors resigned because of deeply held convictions that we should not go in. I did make an effort to advise my workers — members of the Association and officers — very, very carefully all the time of my views, to avoid this happening. I've also got a rather delicate situation with the farmers who, in the horticultural field, feel they will suffer from going into the Market. But by and large, because I've been able to talk to them a lot and have gone out of my way to have special meetings with them, they've tended to go along with the explanations and have not really been very difficult.

But, although nothing much happened in six of the nine cases, in three the stakes were much higher. The Common Market was the issue in two of them, one Labour, one Conservative. In the third a Conservative who is liberal on questions of race confronted a constituency association which was much less so.

An additional disadvantage I suffered from was the element of surprise. I can remember Iain Macleod coming to my Association dinner and saying to them, 'Be loyal to your Member' and all the rest of it: 'The really tough time will come when he kicks over the traces, and that's when you've really got to back up your Member of Parliament and be loyal to him.' And I remember sitting there thinking, 'I'm not the sort of chap who will ever kick over the traces. I'm really the sort of carbon-copy party hack, a loyalist.' And then suddenly this race thing absolutely exploded out of the blue, with Enoch and all the rest of it.

There was a meeting of my local Conservative Council immediately after that, and I had a very rough ride, although somehow it ended without them actually taking a vote. If they had, I suppose there would have been two people out of the fifty or sixty in the room who would have actually supported me on that occasion. But somehow my Chairman and agent – who played it for the unity of the cause – managed to avoid a direct move.

And then there was the committee on the Race Relations Bill, and largely due to the inadequacy of the Labour whipping they were short of people on a key vote which ended up with me to cast the deciding vote. If I had voted for the Conservative amendment, we would have defeated the Government. Instead, I voted with the Labour Party and sustained the Labour Government, and my people were understandably furious. It was on the front page of the *Daily Telegraph*. And my constituents sent a deputation to the Oppostion Chief Whip, who mercifully handled them with great tact and firmness, which was good of him. And then we got into the hard graft and some people began to say, 'Well, you know, we'll have to think about adopting another candidate for the next election. You weren't elected as the Member to do these things against the interests of your constituents.'

In the end this particular Member was readopted but only after he had gone through what he calls 'a very difficult phase'.

The Conservative who got into serious trouble with his constituency association over the Common Market supported the idea of a European free trade area but was opposed to Britain's joining the EEC.

At the last election I put it in my election address, which went to every voter, that I was opposed to our going into the Common Market. During the election I had seventy meetings – public meetings – at which this came up, and I made it absolutely clear where I stood. I was re-elected, and my majority went up by several thousands, which is not bad.

Then, a week after the election, some of the people in my Association suddenly realised that the Member whose victory they had acclaimed would in fact be opposing the Government. And they got very worried that my vote would bring the Government down and so on. And then started a very long battle of ideas and pressures, and I was even asked to stop asking questions [in Parliament] to the Prime Minister about the Common Market. All sorts of curious things – really curious things I must do, which I refused to do.

So there was a bit of a bust-up. The Executive passed a resolution saying they were all in favour of going into the Common Market. I don't know that they were all in favour, but they were panicked that I might bring the Government down. And so it went on, and I consistently voted against the Government on the Common Market and of course the Government wasn't brought down. I'd told them it probably wouldn't be because there were going to be enough Socialists to support the Government anyhow. And I think on that I've been proved right.

At the heart of the relationship between an MP and his constituency party is the constituency party's power to select its parliamentary candidate. Every sitting MP was once adopted as a candidate by his local party or association; and every MP knows that his local party has it in its power to refuse to readopt him at some time in the future. The fact that this power is seldom exercised does not make it any the less real. At one of the Conservative dinners one of the older Members was taking a rather lofty view of his relations with his local people. A newer Member shook his head:

I'm bound to say that — perhaps because I'm more junior — I can't afford to take that sort of line. They are the selectorate: they are the people who decide whether you are going to be the candidate at the election.

A Labour MP who had defied the party whip on the Common Market was of the same opinion.

I used to aim to attend every other meeting of my General Management Committee. I felt that that was about right, and it fitted in with my commitments at Westminster. But since the Common Market I've found myself going to the GMC every month — to protect my position really. If you're in a difficult situation, you've got to cultivate them.

Another Labour Member was even more blunt:

You either get on well with your party or you don't. And if you don't you're going to be dead one day.

Some MPs, however, denied that they thought much about whether or not they would be readopted.

How far do the people sitting round this table maintain good relations with their party activists conscious of the fact that ultimately these people have the power to readopt or not readopt?
No, no, I don't think one's conscious of this at all. Partly because of the enormous conceit we all have, we find it unthinkable that they could ever dream of getting rid of us. But I don't really think that

you can conduct this kind of close relationship with your party over a five-year, ten-year, fifteen-year period, on the basis that you've got to watch what you say here in case you're going to be turfed out. Conflicts arise, but the point is you're less effective if you get out of tune with your own party.

Even those MPs, the majority, who admitted that they were aware of the constituency party's ultimate power denied that, except over very minor matters, they allowed their judgement to be swayed.

This may sound a bit priggish, I'm afraid, but I've always ignored this selectorate business because I reckon that, once you pay attention to your selection next time, your judgement may be affected. Therefore, I ignore the selection question and, when it comes up, I defend myself, you know, as the case may be. And I press on.

I find it inconceivable that I would ever go to my General Management Committee and say, 'Look, there's this business about (say) immigration coming up. What do you think?' I consult them because I don't want to get across them, but on anything important I wouldn't dream of letting them take the lead.

But, although few MPs will succumb to pressure over a single vote or issue, sustained pressure from the constituency could of course over time weaken a Member's will to resist.

Considering the large number of occasions on which MPs and their constituency associations do disagree, it is perhaps surprising that refusals to readopt – or even threats of non-readoption – are not more common. The MPs were generally agreed that one factor that would inhibit a local party was fear of losing a marginal seat.

Why didn't you get into worse trouble?
Well, it's partly that I sit for a highly marginal seat. If you win a marginal seat and then hold it against the swing, you're in a very powerful position: you're an electoral asset locally, and they'll almost certainly lose the seat if they ditch you. Not only that: they'll lay themselves open to criticism for years to come for having precipitated this kind of thing.

Another Tory with a liberal record on race questions – not the one quoted above – was equally clear why he had not been under greater pressure.

Let's not beat about the bush. The only reason I haven't got into trouble with them – or even more trouble than I have – is because I'm in a critically marginal seat. They know that if they threw me over they would be making sure a Conservative wouldn't get elected. I sometimes think the safer the seat the more trouble you get from your association: they think they can run you.

If the threat, even the implicit threat, of not being readopted has to be taken seriously by MPs, they are also in a position to issue a threat of their own. At least two of our Conservatives, both of whom had been in some difficulty, had made it known that if their associations disowned them they would stand as Independents. Their associations could not ignore this possibility. Independents may not often win elections; but a former MP standing as an Independent could well throw the election to the other side. To be sure, he would probably destroy his political career in the process but, once he had been disowned by his supporters, his political career would almost certainly have been destroyed anyway. Certainly, if the two MPs who said they had made this threat were bluffing, their bluff was not called.

They said: 'You've got to vote with the Government because there's going to be a three-line whip.' And I said, 'I'm not going to vote with the Government.' And I didn't. Then there were sort of rumblings, and little noises around, you know: 'Well, we'll have to consider your readoption.' To which I rumbled back in a roundabout sort of way: 'If I'm not readopted for doing what I told the electors I'd do, then I'd be forced, morally, to stand nevertheless – because the issue would be that I was not being readopted simply because of keeping an election promise – and therefore I'd be forced to stand.' As an Independent or Conservative or whatever, you see. Once they hoisted that in, they began to think again: 'That's his way and he'll keep his fight up.' And that, I hope, is the end of the story.

I agree. Whenever the suggestion came up of adopting another candidate, I always took the line: 'I am fighting the next election; you can take that absolutely for granted. Whether or not you support me is entirely up to you.'

Another factor restraining local associations is the general belief in Britain that, on matters about which they feel strongly, MPs should on the whole be free to follow the dictates of their consciences; it was to this belief that Iain Macleod was appealing in the passage quoted earlier. But probably even more important is the great lengths to which most Members go to solicit their supporters' views and generally to attend to their wants. Almost everyone at the dinners agreed that an MP's relationship with his supporters could withstand considerable political disagreement provided his personal relations with them remained good.

The liberal Conservative who ran into trouble over Enoch Powell and the Race Relations Bill felt he had learned a lesson from the experience.

I decided after that that every time Enoch spoke on race – he spoke at regular intervals you'll remember – I would find an opportunity to go to either a ward or a constituency executive committee and explain in a very detailed way why I disagreed with what he had said in his last speech. Slowly but surely they got used to this, and it became, well, not quite a standing joke, but that sort of thing. And by the time the next election came the question of my readoption never came up. Indeed it was seconded by the chairman of the local Monday Club. I'm really just saying that this personal relationship with the constituency Council, and taking the trouble to talk to them and explain, I think in my case was more successful than I would ever have dreamt.

The points about freedom of conscience and good personal relations were also made by a pro-European Labour Member who, despite voting with the Conservative Government in the critical division in October 1971, had not had any trouble.

They disagreed, and two wards sent me telegrams and asked to see me just before the 28 October vote. And I went to see them and said, 'Look, you know I've been in favour of this for a very long time. You can't really expect me to stand on my head.' And they said, 'Well, if you can't actually vote against it, couldn't you just sort of not vote?' And I said, 'Well, you know, really this doesn't make any sense with a major issue of this sort.' And they said, 'Well, no, perhaps it doesn't, so OK.'

The reasons basically why I didn't have any trouble on the Market were because of the relationship one had developed over a decade, which was frankly one of fairly relaxed and mutual tolerance. They were a unilateralist party [i.e. on nuclear disarmament] when they adopted me, and they knew I was a multilateralist. On a large number of issues we disagreed throughout the period of the Labour Government. But we always disagreed on the basis that they never tried to tell me what to do, and I never tried to give a strong political lead to the GMC. On that basis we got on very well.

Something that emerged clearly at the dinners was that MPs keep in touch with their constituency parties largely for the sake of keeping in touch. They go to considerable trouble to solicit their supporters' views and to listen to their opinions. They do so, however, not because they value their constituents' opinions on major national issues (by and large they do not), but because they wish to remain on good terms with them and because they believe that their supporters have, at the very least, a right to be heard. To some extent, too, they listen because they have to: large numbers of meetings with party supporters are part of every MP's life. In the background, as always, is the knowledge that the local party does have the power ultimately to determine the MP's future – and also the knowledge, especially in marginal seats, that if the party workers are too alienated from the Member to go out and work for him the seat may be lost.

One Conservative described how he learned the importance of keeping in touch:

I had a very sharp lesson shortly after I first got in, when I ran slap bang into the virtually solid opposition of my entire constituency Council – the main governing body. And, perhaps because I hadn't really kept in touch with them on a personal level, it was much more difficult for me to pick up the pieces afterwards. The lesson I drew out of that was that, whatever happened in the future, I was going to keep in very close touch with them on a personal level – not so much to get their views, but so that I could always ring up and talk to them.

Another Conservative expressed himself very forcibly:

My Association need guidance. They need, quite frankly, to be told what to think about things. They haven't any views themselves. The ones they have are vague prejudices which they don't – they are not willing to – substantiate. If you tell them the Government has admitted Ugandan Asians and that this is a right and decent thing to do, then they will accept this – although they may have natural tendencies to take a different view altogether.

He added:

I attend a large number of functions run by the local Conservative

Association, but I don't do it in order to learn anything political: I do it to make myself personally acceptable to them so that they will continue to take this general guidance on these sorts of issues.

It was this particular MP's belief that, at least on the Conservative side, constituency associations almost always took their political colouration from the views of their Member: if he was left-wing, they would be; if he was a Powellite, then they would be too.

Another Conservative MP, from a quite different background and sitting for an entirely different sort of constituency, was also clear that in his relations with his local association his aim was to teach, not to learn.

I don't actually live physically in my constituency, but I live in a neighbourhood very similar to the one I represent, and there is no difference between where I live and the problems of my constituency — so I reckon I know them as well as they do. Suppose something is going to come up — a storm-in-a-teacup sort of thing — say everybody is upset because lorries are being parked overnight in residential streets — that sort of thing. Somebody will ring me up and say, 'Look this is coming up on the agenda'; but I will know that because they'll be parking outside my house too. The point is that they're not educating me really about their views because I reckon I know them as well as anybody else. Most of their views anyway will be culled from the pages of the *Daily Telegraph* and the *Daily Express*. I'm talking about the Association members. As long as one reads those papers anyway, one would know what their reactions were going to be. What I do is to contrive to meet people in houses around the constituency. I get somebody to say, 'Right, invite a few friends in for drinks one evening.' And they come in for drinks, and I talk for five minutes, and then they just shoot at me. The practical effect is to sell me and my views — not, to be utterly frank, to educate me about the views of people in the Association.

The same MP added later that he does pay attention to the views of his Association but does not trim towards them.

Few of the Labour Members expressed themselves quite as forcibly, but what they said in most cases amounted to the same thing. 'I see my job', one of them said flatly, 'as politically educating my constituency.' Another recalled the time of the Labour Government:

The only time I ever felt an obligation to consult about national issues was when I used to go to every GMC, every monthly Management Committee meeting. I would spend about a quarter of an hour attempting to explain the variations that had taken place that month in Government policy. [*Laughter*]. This was not always fruitful as far as the Government was concerned, but it was terribly useful as far as the members of the GMC were concerned. At least they felt they had some kind of – oh, I don't know – some kind of conduit pipe through which their grievances could be passed up. I think that's worth saying.

A sense of involvement.

Yes, a sense of involvement. It's terribly important, particularly when you're doing things you know they don't like.

All this applies to national politics. On local matters, however, the MPs were prepared to take advice and often intervened as, in effect, referees in constituency disputes. A Labour MP remarked:

As far as local issues are concerned, if the borough council, which is Labour-controlled, is going to do something, as indeed they do quite frequently, rent schemes or redevelopment schemes, which are bitterly offensive to a large chunk of the Labour voters in the borough, well then obviously one spends a considerable amount of time either trying to modify it, or what you couldn't modify you could at least try to explain to the party members.

I had a good full-time agent, and I don't think a week ever passed when I didn't talk to him at least two or three times. This was to get advice which would help me as to what I should do in the local party and also to talk to him about local issues.

The techniques MPs employ for keeping in touch with their local party activists vary greatly from person to person. Drinks parties in people's houses, telephone calls to one's agent, have been mentioned already. On the Conservative side there is something of a pattern.

How do you go about keeping in touch with opinion in the party in the constituency – not the voters at large – but with your own people? What actually do you do?

Well, I do it principally through my chief officers – through my Chairman, through my President, who is active, through my agent, through the chairman of the Women's Advisory Committee, through one or two of the officers in the Young Conservatives. Now that sounds almost too good to be true, but it does in fact work out that way, although I do take soundings from other people. I've got a half-rural constituency and I have to make a point of seeing farmers — some of them are officers in the Association. Only this week, for example, something has come up about the Government's possibly taking off the quota on apple imports, which is a very sensitive thing indeed in my constituency, and I've seen a number of farmers about this in order to be able to speak to the Minister.

Do the people in the Association ring you up or do you ring them?

Very often they ring me up at home or write to me, or my agent, who is a very experienced man, warns me of things that are brewing or worrying people. Ugandan Asians was a typical one. And in fact — this will amuse my colleagues — but it was my wife who rang me up when she was away herself and said, 'You will have to do something about this Ugandan Asian problem.' So I said, 'Why should I?' This was in the recess and she said, 'I'm sure this is the sort of thing that will disturb them.' Well, we don't have a single coloured immigrant in my constituency, but it stirred people up a great deal nevertheless, and I made a point on that of taking soundings from other people and of putting out statements.

Presumably you spend quite a lot of time attending formal party meetings of one kind or another - and social functions?

Yes, I do. I'm invited to my divisional Executive which meets six times a year. I'm not automatically there, but I'm invited to come along to the whole meeting to listen to the things that are going on in the constituency administratively and so on — things that are on their minds. And then I address them afterwards and answer questions. That's a regular way in which I can keep in touch. Of course that's a central Association thing. More informally I have a practice whereby I attend all — well, pretty well all — my branch Annual General Meetings; and on top of this there are a lot of other meetings that I attend, some of which are social, and some discussion groups.

Oh yes, one other thing. We have in the rural areas what we call cottage meetings, when it's not in a village hall, where someone throws their house open and gives some sort of a coffee evening — maybe even a glass of wine or something like that. It's not so bad as some would think because you have a lot of talkback on those occasions. You don't make much of a speech — maybe five minutes and then a lot of questions afterwards. But sometimes on these occasions — it's left to the person locally — people will be invited who are not members of the party, and I remember once saying, 'The Tories seemed a bit restive tonight', and my wife said to me afterwards, 'Well, they weren't Tories. Don't you realise that all parties were there tonight? The village postman is a Socialist.' I had to admit I didn't realise that.

Another Tory, sitting for a compact constituency near the centre of a large city, had a somewhat different story to tell.

I happen to live right in the middle of my constituency geographically, and one tends naturally to come into contact with the leading party workers — just by the very fact that you're there. We don't have any formal relationship in the sense that (say) I attend the Executive Committee every other Tuesday — though if they have a meeting and I'm there, for example, during the recess, then I'll go. I do have one thing that I find very successful, and that is that I send out a monthly newsletter — literally on the first day of each month, to the leading party workers: the branch chairman, councillors, people like that — which really tells them what I'm doing, attending these dinners for example. And they're very interested, you know, and they ask me, 'What are they about?' This helps me.

What about the telephone? Do you get rung up very much?

No. This is one thing about actually living right in the middle of the constituency. If I minded people knocking at my door at 7 o'clock in the morning, I wouldn't live there. But I do have an ex-directory number: I'm not having drunks ringing up at 3 o'clock in the morning. If I was married, then I might think of not having an ex-directory number and my wife could answer it.

Then you could have more drunks ringing up in the middle of the night.

Contacts on the Labour side tend to be more casual, although, like the Conservatives, most Labour MPs do try to attend fairly regularly their local governing body — in the Labour case their General Management Committee. A Northern Labour MP remarked:

My contact with the party supporters really is in a very workaday way. One way is this: my regular weekly surgery takes place in one of the two Labour clubs in my constituency, where inevitably each week I meet a number of the party workers. As far as party meetings are concerned, I have very few. The only really regular one is my quarterly GMC, which anyway very rarely gets round to discussing politics. You know how it is: by the time we've finished discussing the minutes of the last meeting, time's already dragging on.

I very rarely get rung up. Sometimes a particular party officer calls me — the secretary obviously, but also particular individuals whose judgement I've come to rely on. I have a constituency that's quite widespread, and there are quite a number of local parties, so I've got to rely on different people whom I can contact, or who I can rely on to contact me if any difficulties are likely.

Are these people – the ones you rely on – people who necessarily hold
some official position in the local party?
Usually. Usually but certainly not invariably.

This MP was not the only one on the Labour side who
seemed to depend quite heavily on a network of personal contacts, sometimes consisting of only two or three individuals.
Another Northern Member said that there were only two
people in his constituency with whom he would discuss actual
political issues:

I value their judgement – the fact that they will know what feeling is
in the area. If I'm asked to a particular meeting and am not sure what
the atmosphere is going to be, or how important the attitudes are on
a particular issue that has blown up, I may sometimes ring them up
and discuss it with them. I certainly regard these two persons as
having far and away the most incisive political judgement in the
constituency, and I am mostly in touch with them.

Much of the discussion at the dinners – especially about
MPs who had been in trouble with their local association or
party – was based on the assumption that most leading party
activists would be likely to be 'political', in the sense of having
strongly-held views about major political questions. This assumption is often made in the press and, somewhat less often,
in the academic literature. But several of the MPs at the dinners went out of their way to report that on the basis of their
own experience party activists seemed little concerned about
the big national issues and either were not interested in issues
at all or else were interested only in local matters. One Conservative insisted:

Mine is a non-political Association. This is my experience – I put it
no higher than that, and I accept that other people may have found
differently – but I think it's true that most people who join the Conservative Party are non-political: they wish to join some organisation
that will do something; they are Conservatives in a moderate sort of
way. Their only strong political views are that Conservatism should
be expressed through loyalty to the party, its leaders and its policies.
As long as they are told about this and what these are, then they will
follow on.

Another Conservative agreed that he had 'a pretty a-political
Association'. But a third had had an entirely different ex-

perience and was rather surprised by what the other two had said.

This is certainly not so in my constituency, where there's one over-riding political issue and that's coloured immigration. And because of that, I've found, people become concerned with the environment, law and order — you name it. In fact they're deeply concerned politically: they certainly don't treat politics as a social thing.

And the same variation was evident on the Labour side. The Labour MPs were asked whether their General Management Committees were on the whole anxious to talk politics.

My constituency party is very keen on national politics.

Mine isn't. Personalities are much more important.

Highly political mine.

I certainly haven't got what could be described as a virulently political GMC.

Political, but locally oriented.

Half is highly political, and half of it isn't.

Clearly, other things being equal, an MP with a highly political local association or party would stand a greater chance of coming into conflict with his supporters over matters like the Common Market or race relations. But why some associations should be more political than others, in this sense, did not emerge.

Most of what was said about the MP/constituency party relationship could have been said by MPs of either party. The differences within the parties were greater than the differences between them. Two points of contrast are, however, worth singling out: one having to do with how Members keep in touch, the other with the status that MPs accord their supporters' views.

Readers may already have noticed that, in the discussion about how one keeps in touch, the Labour Members did not seem to have any single normal channel of communication, while the Conservatives tended to mention the holders of the formal party offices in their constituencies. This contrast emerged again and again in the course of the conversations, one Conservative going so far as to say:

A very experienced constituency officer told me before I was accepted for my present constituency – a man who, incidentally, had been chairman of a division for about twenty-four years – he gave me this advice: 'All you have to do is to make sure that you retain the loyalty and the support of four people: your President, your Chairman, the chairman of your Women's Advisory, and your agent – four people – that's all you've got to do.'

This was something that no Labour MP would have said, yet most of the other Conservatives present nodded their agreement.

As far as the officers are concerned, the explanation is probably that once officers have been elected on the Conservative side they are largely allowed to run the association and to speak for it; they are allowed to get on with it. An MP who keeps on good terms with his officers is therefore, to a large extent, keeping on good terms with his association as a whole. On the Labour side, by contrast, General Management Committees are reluctant to surrender any of their prerogatives to the party officers, with the result that the MP has to pay attention to the GMC as a whole and therefore to its more influential members, whoever they may be.

As regards the position of the agent, his potential power is probably about the same in both parties. The agent, if he is full-time, is usually the one man who devotes the whole of his time and energy to the local party's affairs and is in touch with all sections of opinion. As a Conservative put it:

If your agent has to be persuaded on every issue to accept your point of view – if in the end he often doesn't accept it – then the Member's position is very, very difficult, unhappy and possibly even untenable. The agent is all-powerful really. He's there seven days a week working, and of course appointing all the constituency officers virtually – arranging their appointments – he can fix it. He can whisper; he can do all sorts of things. He's a very, very powerful person indeed.

The same Member added:

If you have an agent who is intelligent and well-educated, as I have, who has himself aspired to be a Member of Parliament, and who is capable of thinking every bit as intelligently as a Member of Parliament, then it is essential to overcome what could be a hurdle in a social relationship – to avoid the chip on the shoulder.

Moreover, as another Conservative pointed out, although the agent may have some say in the election of the officers, in the end he works for them: he is the association's servant. And, since he is not the MP's servant (the MP neither appoints him nor pays him), in a crisis he is more likely to side with the association than with the Member. This particular MP had once had this experience:

My agent, curiously enough, was at first very loyal. He had been a chief petty officer in the Navy and naturally was very loyal, as you would expect a chief petty officer to be. Then the Powell thing came up. I said some rude things about Powell, but my Association thought he was a great man. The agent was faced with the issue: 'Do I support the Member, or do I support the Chairman?' And it came down to the fact that of course he's paid by the Association, by the Chairman, and therefore he supported the Chairman and the Association and, in my absence in London, he went round to branches sowing dissension against me. It made life very difficult for a time.

Several Labour MPs also testified to the agent's potential power. Where the two parties differ is not in the role of the agent as such but in the number of their full-time agents. At the time of the dinners, in late 1972, the Conservative Party employed 420 full-time professional agents – that is, with a good deal of sharing, one for almost every constituency in the country – whereas the Labour Party employed only 127. Of the nineteen Members who took part in the dinners, all nine Conservatives had full-time agents but only three of the ten Labour Members. Were the Labour Party ever to employ more full-time agents, it might be that the role of the Labour agent would become considerably more important, and that most Labour MPs, like most Conservatives, would come to regard their agent as a force to be reckoned with – potentially at least.

The other point of contrast between the parties is connected with what was said earlier about MPs of both parties listening to their constituents' views on national questions not so much because they expect to learn from them – or feel any obligation to heed them – but because they wish to remain on good terms with them. Although all of the Conservatives present and almost all of the Labour MPs held broadly this view, one or two Labour Members said things which implied that their conception was rather different. One agreed with the others that he would not be content simply 'to reflect the political attitudes prevailing in the constituency' but went on to say:

To me it's the movement I represent – the Labour movement. On the big political questions, yes, I am influenced by discussions with political people – that is, with the movement – with the constituency party as well as the Labour Party in the House.

Certainly members of the Tribune Group claim that Members of Parliament should on occasion be prepared to sacrifice their own judgement to that of the Labour movement as a whole; but whether in practice they behave any differently from their colleagues it is hard to say, since most Tribune Group MPs anyway represent constituencies where the local Labour party holds the same views as they do.

For a variety of reasons MPs cultivate good relations with their party supporters. But the question arises: in keeping in touch with their own party activists, how far are they also keeping in touch with their constituents at large – with the people in their constituency, the great majority, who do not belong to a political party and probably never attend a party meeting? One Conservative Member was adamant that there might be a conflict between the two and that, if he paid over-much attention to the views of his party stalwarts, he would be in danger of giving too little weight to the views of ordinary voters, especially of the ordinary voters who voted for him.

At the last election I got somewhere in the order of twenty thousand votes. Now the membership of our Conservative Association is claimed to be about two thousand. Therefore, in my opinion it is not so much what the Association members think that matters as what the grass roots, who are all the others, really think. I draw a very clear distinction in my own mind between the two, because I regard quite a few of the members of my Association, particularly the officers, as being servile, because all they want is that one should be loyal to the party – to the leader really. So I know what the reactions of my officers are going to be: 'You must support Mr Heath, full stop.' And therefore I concentrate much more on what the balance of the Tory voters are thinking.

This MP went on to describe the steps he takes – large numbers of small meetings, coffee mornings, and so – to make sure that grass-roots opinion is not neglected.

But most of the MPs were not as conscious of this potential conflict — or, if they were, did not say so in quite these terms. What most of them did insist on was that contact with party supporters was only one means, and not necessarily the most important one, of finding out what people in the country were thinking and what their problems were. A Labour Member was describing the advantages of attending his General Management Committee.

The one thing that a GMC does, and going to it regularly does, is to bring one down from Westminster and back to earth. I think it's terribly good, frankly, that one has to go to them.

But another Labour MP, although he agreed that it was no bad thing to attend one's GMC, thought it was not nearly so important.

It is one way of being brought down to earth, but my gosh it's not the only thing. This is something we are doing all the time at home, and I would firmly challenge the suggestion that we live in a remote ivory castle at Westminster and only occasionally, when we meet our GMC, do we meet real people. We're meeting them all the time. We live, at home, reasonably normal lives, and we're being challenged the whole time.

And the view on the Tory side was the same.

I don't agree with the view that we're exceptional persons, locked away at Westminster like monks in a cloistered seminary or something. We're not. Most of us live in our constituencies, and one is concerned to know people's views about simple things — not political policies but the cost of living. If you can't identify with the problem of living on £24 a week, then you're not a very successful Member of Parliament.

Surely the thing is that, even without keeping in touch with your constituency, you know what their views are on the cost of living. You live a fairly ordinary life yourself, and your ordinary social contacts tell you that. I reckon I'm just as aware of these sorts of issues as my constituents are.

As the last few paragraphs make clear, any discussion of the MP's relationship with his party supporters is bound to broaden into a discussion of his relationship with his constituency in general. His party supporters are concerned, among other things, to tell him what his other constituents are thinking. But the two subjects are different all the same. One can imagine, for example, an MP who was on bad terms with his party supporters but was highly regarded by his constituents at large. More to the point, much of the work that an MP does for his constituency is done on a non-party basis and would be done even if such things as local Conservative associations and Labour parties ceased to exist. For these reasons, the largely non-partisan aspects of MPs' constituency work were discussed separately at the Granada dinners. They are also discussed separately here.

3 Working for the Constituency

Members of Parliament are expected to perform two kinds of services for their constituencies. In the first place, they are expected to concern themselves with the individual problems of their constituents: with regard to housing, employment, pensions – with regard to almost anything. In this connection, most MPs hold weekly or fortnightly 'surgeries' in their constituencies; that is, they make themselves available in a municipal office, village hall or some such place, and constituents can come along and talk to them personally. MPs also receive dozens of letters each week about similar problems of an essentially individual sort.

In the second place, MPs are expected to attend to the more collective wants of their constituencies: to prevent the closing of this factory or that hospital, to secure the inclusion in the building programme of a long-sought bypass or sewage works, to settle an industrial dispute in a local factory. These activities can also generate a large volume of correspondence, as well as necessitating the issuing of statements, the holding of meetings with constituents, local authority officials and ministers, and perhaps even interventions in the House of Commons.

All the MPs who attended the Granada dinners took their constituency work seriously. None of them shirked it or regarded it as anything less than very important. Nevertheless, they admitted to spending extraordinarily different proportions of their time on it. The MPs were asked to estimate roughly the percentage of their total working time they devoted to constituency work: attending surgeries, answering letters, and so on. The response of the first Labour Member to reply clearly amazed his colleagues.

Difficult to quantify obviously, but I would say eight-tenths to nine-tenths of my time.
Eight to nine tenths!

Eight to nine tenths.
Good God.

Most Members, Conservative and Labour, volunteered a figure in the range of from twenty-five to forty per cent, but some, again on both sides of the House, spent less. Another Labour Member startled his colleagues not by how much time he spent on constituency business but by how little.

I would say that my time per week is (say) two meetings, apart from attending surgeries once a week, four visits, and (say) two hours of dictation per week.
Is that all?
On purely constituency work, yes.
Two hours?!

In absolute terms, the amount of work put in by many MPs is prodigious, though Members who devote the most time to the political side of their lives do not necessarily spend a particularly large proportion of it on their constituencies.

I calculated, when I was looking into the question for the Boyle commission on salaries and so on, that I was spending sixty-five to seventy hours a week on my political activities: constituency, in Parliament, and so on. And I think certainly a quarter of that is on constituency matters.

While he's been talking, I've just been doing the calculation. I average myself, on a time and motion study, to work eighty-two hours a week when Parliament is sitting. Of that, I reckon I spend eighteen hours on constituency matters – on their letters, on their problems, and meeting them in the constituency. That's – what? – just under a fifth of my time.

This Member calculated that from Mondays to Thursdays, when he was at the House, he spent about two hours a day on constituency matters. A colleague interjected:

Two hours? That's not so much. I mean I spent three hours alone on the phone today talking to bloody fools at the other end.

There are all sorts of reasons why one MP may devote more time to his constituency than another. The distance between Westminster and the Member's constituency is one factor – the London MPs, for instance, seemed to spend less time on their constituencies than the others – and so is whether the constituency is physically compact, like most urban divisions, or scattered, like most constituencies in East Anglia or rural Scotland. And some constituencies — say, urban ones with declining industries — present more problems than others. Some MPs are more efficient than others, and some undoubtedly work harder. It takes a very conscientious MP to go to the trouble, for example, that this Labour man did.

You have to allow time for reading the letters — the eight-page letter, for instance, from an old lady the other day, writing about an electricity account — that I have to read. It took me an hour to transcribe that letter. I had to write down every single word I could not decipher at first, because deep in the body of that letter — amid all the irrelevancies about what a nice chap her husband was, and the lovely house they used to have in Jersey — deep in the body of that letter was the fact that she was being summonsed for non-payment of this account. And the thing was urgent, so I couldn't afford to skimp that letter. I really had to decipher it.

The overwhelming impression left by the dinners was that most MPs on both sides do the same sorts of constituency work, and do it in the same sorts of ways. Disagreement was mainly over details. One Conservative Member, to the considerable surprise of the others, insisted that the only surgeries worth holding were ones where constituents came by prior appointment:

I do the kind without appointments purely as a public relations exercise — that I'm available to the public. But I get all the dregs of society, and in fact it's largely a waste of time. People who take the trouble to ring up and make an appointment — they may not have a case, they may have one, but at least they don't just wander in for lack of anything better to do.

I don't agree at all. I would say there's a lot of time taken up doing it the way I do it, but I've had a significant number of what I would call successes and a great many letters of thanks, and that's a fact.

Another Conservative, to the even greater surprise of his colleagues, announced that he did not hold surgeries at all.

I've stopped them. My predecessor had surgeries every Monday morning — if you can think of a more depressing time to have a surgery. [*Loud laughter*]. I inherited this system, and it meant there were about twenty regulars. I mean they'd come in — they'd miss a couple of months and then they'd pick up the theme again – and I found that I was spending my Monday mornings over a year with the same few people telling me their stories and fantasies and so on. The genuine cases were squeezed out by the regulars.

So I decided to stop this, and I advertised in the local paper that I would have an evening surgery, with a local councillor in attendance, and we ran it for six weeks and not a single person turned up. Not a single person. So I went back to Monday mornings [*laughter*] and tried it for another stint, and then I just gave it up. It was very largely a waste of time.

This Member sits for a London constituency and has a fairly large staff. His arrangement now is that, if someone definitely wants to see him, he can make an appointment and come along to the House of Commons, which is only a short distance away.

Almost every MP can recall one or two constituency cases of which he is particularly proud, either because he achieved something that was important to the individual concerned or because the case was an especially tricky one. When the Labour Members were asked whether they could think of any particular cases, one of them called out, 'That's not a question, that's an invitation.' At the Conservative dinner, someone said *sotto voce*, 'Come on boys, let's have it.' Two or three of the stories are worth repeating.

One that comes to my mind was someone who had been employed by the Post Office and had had a personality clash with his technical supervisor, as the result of which he gradually broke down, was transferred to another branch, had an accident and couldn't continue to travel to the other branch, and became unemployed. His relations with his employer gradually grew worse and worse.

By the time he came to see me, he'd been unemployed for nearly two years. He was aged 56, but he didn't want to retire, though the Post Office wanted prematurely to retire him on medical grounds. And it was partly a problem because he also alienated people: he developed very difficult personality traits. He alienated his trade union secretary, the district secretary of more than one branch, and so he could get no help there, and he was becoming distinctly paranoid.

It was a matter of seeing the local union officials, seeing local employers, writing to the head of the Post Office. And finally, after receiving a number of encouraging letters and compromises that were

very much less than what he wanted, I went to see one of the top
people in the Post Office, and as the result of that interview he was
given, at a lower grade, his old job back. And as the result of that — it
sounds, when I talk about it, very much like a fairy story — he has
become, as one says, an entirely new man.

I can think of one case of an old bloke who came to see me to see if
we could increase his pension. We tried everything, but there was no
basis at all for increasing his pension. Then I happened to ask him
what was wrong with his arm, and it seemed he'd got it wounded in
the 1914-18 War and his pension was computed in 1922. So he got
paid a lump sum: in the end the Ministry of Defence went right back
to 1922 and we got him an extra 12s 6d a week — fifty years back.

The most satisfactory one I had was a woman who came to me and
complained that the then Metropolitan Commissioner of Police — who was it? — Sir John Waldron and Rab Butler were running
the brothels of London [*raucous laughter*] and moreover that all the
drug manufacturers were in a conspiracy with Rab Butler and Sir
John Waldron to try and keep this dreadful secret quiet, and were
polluting all the medicines that were given to her. And, after I reported this to the Prime Minister, it all stopped [*laughter*] and it was
a very successful operation.

Almost certainly the postal worker, the pensioner and the
woman all believed that their MP's intervention had been
decisive. But at one of the Labour dinners the question was
raised of how far MPs really do assist their constituents; after
all, it could be argued that in most cases the outcome would be
the same even if no one intervened or alternatively that, although someone may need to intervene, it need not be an MP.
The expression of this latter view by one young Member started a rather heated argument.

Let's face it: in most individual cases somebody else could have done
it. There are some individual cases where nobody but the MP could
have done it, but in most somebody else could have.
No, no. Absolutely wrong.
Right.
No. First of all, take local councillors for instance: they don't feel ade-
quate to the machine: secondly, they may not be able to figure out which
is the right bit of the machine; the third thing is that they do not have
the MP's cachet. Now, if you've been in government departments, as
some of us here have, you know that letters come in from MPs, and you
look at them and you say, 'That dum-dum has written a letter about

so-and-so.' And to your astonishment, because he's an MP, his letter is given a green folder, it's flagged Urgent – it's got a signal on it saying, 'For God's sake, answer this tomorrow.'
No, I'm sorry, a large number of cases that Members take up could have been adequately dealt with by a person who was not a Member. All that is required is for the person to know his arse from his elbow so far as the administrative machine is concerned, and to get the case out of the low level where it's being dealt with to a slightly higher level. There are exceptions, of course, but in general the MP really isn't needed.

Some Members, in the course of the same discussion, also expressed doubts about the ethics of the MP's role, especially in housing cases.

What we have most of the time in housing is a quite inappropriate use of the Member of Parliament. It is to try to jump the bureaucratic queue, and to go outside the criteria, which ought to be standard and which ought to operate in an entirely impartial manner. And one is being constantly asked to interfere with this process, I suspect often by the people who know how to pull strings and not those in the greatest need at all.
Yes, it's perfectly possible that someone has been correctly dealt with by the machine, and according to the rules something has been decided. Now, if you then in that circumstance use the position of an MP to get him favoured treatment, I think this is wrong.

On the other hand, it may be easier to write a letter to (say) the local housing manager than to give the constituent a frosty answer face to face.
   The one thing that everyone seemed agreed on was that work on individual cases of this kind is not done primarily to win votes. One London Member in fact was at pains to assert the contrary proposition:

I'm quite certain that my surgery loses me votes rather than gains them.
How?
Because those people for whom I get something must be ten per cent of the total – because most of them come to me as housing cases. And I cannot do it bingo, but they come to me anyway. They either don't deserve to get what they want, or they haven't got a cat in hell's chance of getting it whether they deserve it or not. And you lose those people because you don't get them what they think they're

entitled to. You only gain those few people who feel, well, you failed
but you tried.

The same Member added, ironically:

Everybody for whom I get a house gets one outside my constituency,
so there's a happy ring of my supporters around London. Those who
are left are those for whom I failed.

MPs admit to getting a certain amount of personal satisfaction from successful individual cases, but most of them
seemed prouder of things they had managed to achieve, not for
individuals, but for their constituencies as a whole. Even those
who doubted whether an MP's intervention is decisive – or
should be decisive – in most individual cases were agreed that
there are certain bigger things that only the Member can do.

I'm very much involved in this sort of thing – getting industrial
development certificates for factory or office development against an
unwilling Government. Sometimes it's taken a year, and it doesn't
matter which Government: whether it's Labour or Tory the fight is
just as hard. Getting roads, bypasses into the programme – new jobs
and so on. I would say this takes up about a quarter of the time I
give to the constituency. One finds oneself writing to ministers, initiating adjournment debates, issuing press statements – all sorts of
things, speaking to the press, bringing it in, constantly finding new
arguments to support one's case.

A Conservative MP told in some detail the story of a constituency campaign that had succeeded – and not just for his
own constituency.

I had a surgery in a market town and five ladies came to see me from
a little country village, and they said, 'Do you know that Mrs Smith,
our village schoolmistress, has got to leave?' And I said, 'No.' They
said, 'Haven't you seen the Ministry of Education instruction?' And I
said, 'No, because we don't see them as MPs.'
   They then showed me what it was, and it was that, unless a school
teacher had got a qualification, she must go; in other words, all school
teachers must be qualified. Mrs Smith had been there for twenty
years and was a marvellous teacher. Everyone in the village loved
her, and her products – her pupils – were perfect in the way they
went on to higher schools and so on, and they said, 'We want to keep
her.'
   So that was the first time I'd heard of this rule of the last Government that all teachers have to be qualified. So I took this up, and I

went to see the Minister of Education, Short, who said, 'No, no. No change.'

I put down questions in the House but got no satisfaction. I then started a press campaign, writing to the *Telegraph*. I then had an adjournment debate and I got a number of other colleagues to take part, demanding that these unqualified teachers of fifteen or twenty years' standing should be allowed to carry on. No joy.

We then went to see, as a delegation, the Minister and eventually we persuaded him to change his mind. In the end, if you'd been teaching for fifteen years or more without a qualification, that was good enough, and the old village schoolmistress could stay on, and then the instruction that went out from the Ministry to all local education authorities was altered, simply because this little delegation of five women came to see me. That started the ball rolling and it rolled all the way.

The only 'spectacular' success one Labour Member claimed concerned the possible loss of a shipbuilding order for his constituency:

three vessels totalling three million pounds, and lots of electronic research likely to go with it. It hinged on a question of credit: the availability of credit to ships built in British yards. And time was of the essence. The order was about to be lost in a matter of days.

It came to me, interestingly, not originally from the management but from the trade union lads. I confirmed it with the management and asked them if they wanted me to act, and they said yes. I took it up – telephoned the Minister, because there was no time to write letters on this. And coincidentally it happened that the Government – our Government then – was about to introduce a new scheme, to change the credit arrangements, which would benefit them.

Obviously the Minister, who was about to announce it, couldn't tell me what it was, but he gave me a hint. And I was able to give them a hint and to tell them to play for time for a matter of days. Which they did. They got the order as a result. The role of the Member there is just simply being able to transmit a nod or a wink.

Mind you, ironically, that firm did not trouble – in contrast with the pensioners and old ladies – did not trouble to write and say thank you to me for it. It was only a mere three million pounds order that they were able to hold onto.

Most men and women who have the same sort of work load as MPs –business executives, lawyers, higher civil servants – are well provided with staff to help them: at the very

least a full-time secretary, probably also a personal assistant of
some sort. Most people not familiar with the House of Commons probably imagine that MPs are well provided for too.
They are not. A Conservative remarked:

I had thirty schoolboys going round the House yesterday, and I was
taking them through the lobby, and they saw a desk with a whole lot
of correspondence and writing paper there, and I said, 'You know,
Members of Parliament write their own letters, and only four years
ago we had to pay for all our own postage.' They were amazed: 'No!'
they said. 'And only two years ago we had to pay for all our own
telephone calls.' 'No!' These were sixteen-year-olds and they couldn't
believe that this was the way things were done only two years ago.

Most of the MPs at the dinners have a staff of one-half: that
is to say, they employ only a part-time secretary, usually based
in London. Some have full-time secretaries, whose salaries
they presumably make up out of their own incomes since the
£1000 allowance they receive for secretarial assistance is clearly not enough. A few have more help, some of it voluntary,
some paid; sometimes it is paid for by their constituency association or trade union. A Conservative Member for a relatively
prosperous constituency is particularly well endowed.

I have a deputy agent, a woman who enjoys going out and meeting
people and talking to people. So, if I get a semi-literate letter, the
deputy agent goes and interviews whoever wrote it. I also have a
chap who acted as my personal assistant in the last election, who's a
Samaritan and who spends perhaps one evening a week, or sometimes
two evenings, also going out and talking to people on my behalf and
is very good at this – in fact on really tricky problems he's absolutely
first-class. And then I have a secretary who spends quite a lot of time
on the phone talking to constituents and so on.

Different Members make very different use of whatever
help they have. The Conservative with the woman deputy
agent and the Samaritan delegates the greater part of his constituency work to them: 'The work is done, but not by me.' He
sees relatively few constituents himself and, although all the
letters that go out over his name are signed by him, most are
drafted by one of his helpers. The Tory Member for a partly
rural constituency, by contrast, was quite clear that he and he
alone should do the work.

I don't believe in using anyone else at all. I deliberately don't let my agent do any work whatsoever in looking after constituents. He's often asked me if he could and I've said no deliberately – not because he's not a competent and very intelligent man, but because I want them to feel that they are being dealt with by their Member of Parliament.

How an MP uses the time of his secretary or other assistants is to some extent a matter of personal taste. One will wish to involve her in the details of his work; another will use her more or less as a pure shorthand/typist. But, as the last quotation suggests ('I want them to feel they are being dealt with by their Member'), the question of staff, which may seem purely administrative on the face of it, in fact raises general questions about what the role of the MP should be. One Member was appalled by the number of hours his colleagues put in on constituency correspondence.

I find the amount of time some of you say you spend totally incredible. I spend perhaps twenty minutes a day signing letters.

He went on to point out that for an MP time is a scarce resource.

Look, this is the real trouble. The whole thing is done on a totally amateur basis. It's ludicrous that people should hang around dictating letters to their secretaries on the vast majority of issues that come from constituents. Ninety-five per cent of the things that come from constituents are of a standard character, have standard considerations involved, have a standard destination. The whole thing can be routine. A lot of one's parliamentary work does require very hard work, because there aren't the research facilities available. But this part of it can be rationalised, and I've rationalised it.

One of the reasons why this particular MP deals with his constituency correspondence in this way is because he does have other things to do – things he regards as more important, given that his secretary is so well able to cope. (Several of the other Members wanted to know where he had found his secretary and how much he paid her.) But, in addition, in many cases involving such things as individual entitlements, claims and complaints – and these cover a broad range of constituency work – he does not feel that he himself has the expertise or the information to be certain whether a central government department or a public corporation has done the right thing or not. Accordingly he was one of a number of Members, on both sides, who made out a strong case for having additional staff – either for themselves or for backbenchers in general.

Suppose I get a letter, and it seems there's a possibility that whoever's written it has been wrongly dealt with. Now, to determine whether he's been wrongly dealt with, you need a certain expertise in a variety of fields, which the Member doesn't necessarily have, which a staff might have. It might be able to build up experience very effectively indeed, and if that were the case I would say that it would be very much better to have such a staff doing that job, checking on the operation of the bureaucracy, than having a Member who, in the field with which the constituent is concerned, might be a total amateur.

An older Member at the same dinner agreed.

The real danger at the present moment lies in the point about expertise that we've just heard. There are certain things where we can come to a quick decision: we know a minister's wrong and we can push on it. But there are others where MPs become a kind of post office: something comes from the constituency; we put it up to the minister; we get a reply – and we haven't got sufficient expertise to look for the flaw.

And he went on to make a further point.

A staff person could make the quick contact that you sometimes need to make with local offices, and for that matter with the local constituent – someone who could actually go there, either to the offices or to the constituent, at times when we can't go. It's sometimes speed that really does matter for an MP: the eviction case, for example.

This MP felt that there should be in each constituency an MP's agent, paid for out of public funds – 'not, you understand, a *political* agent but the *MP's* agent.'

Most of the MPs at the dinners were at least vaguely sympathetic towards the idea of having more staff. Indeed most of them were prepared to set out their requirements.

I'd love to have a secretary available, for whom I hadn't got to pay, in my constituency. That's all I'd ask for.

I would like to have a full-time assistant. I have a secretary in London, but I would like a full-time assistant in London, alongside my office and secretary, to look after my constituency work.

If I had the choice of one extra member of staff, I'd have a trained social worker in my constituency, operating on cases that I referred, or that my contacts referred, to him or her.

I'd opt for moving from the situation of having a part-time secretary here to having a full-time secretary in London and a part-time one in the constituency. I do feel quite seriously that my effectiveness as a Member of Parliament is impeded by the fact that I just haven't the time to follow things up.

But, although this was the general view, one or two MPs were sceptical.

I don't believe that in order to do one's job as the welfare officer for one's constituency – which is what we're talking about – you need a great deal in the way of services. I find I'm perfectly capable of doing it by holding a surgery fairly regularly, by keeping in touch with the constituency party, and by having a very efficient, competent and indeed independent secretary. Perhaps I'm wrong about this, but this is how I've worked for eight years and it seems to me that I'm performing on that side of things reasonably well.

And at least two Members were more than sceptical: they were hostile. One of them insisted:

It's very important not to place between the Member physically and the members of the public a secretary and a staff and, as some people have suggested, a parliamentary office. Because you would then make a Member of Parliament like a minister, where people write to him and the letter gets seen by his staff but probably never by him. I say to my constituents, 'There is one thing about the MP that is different from everybody else. When you write to me, *I* do it. *I* literally do it.'

But most of his colleagues disagreed:

Far from extra staff acting as a barrier, where the MP is a bad MP it might actually help, and where the MP is a good one it could improve the nature of his service and in fact act as a contact, rather than a barrier, between himself and the constituency.

If we had more staff, more advice, more assistance, I don't think I would lose touch. I hope I wouldn't. It would be up to me to ensure that people weren't getting between me and my constituents.

You are not kept less in touch if you have a staff: you are kept more in touch, because you're able to deal more effectively with more problems and more people.

If the majority of MPs at the dinners was typical in very much wanting additional help, why does Parliament not simply vote to provide it? After all, MPs are amongst the few people who, in the end, wholly control their own pay and conditions. A Conservative replied:

You may well ask. Certainly, when I say anything in my constituency about facilities, they say, 'You have the power to do it. Don't grumble to us. Do it.' The trouble is that we're at a point in the development of Parliament where the balance of power still lies with people who have a different concept of what Parliament is about than most of the people around this table. Perhaps in an election or two's time the balance will have changed and we'll see Parliament considered as a full-time job of work that needs to be done with proper back-up. We have to accept that at the moment a lot of our colleagues don't see it that way and resent any suggestion that it should be; and any outward sign that it's becoming that way is resisted.

The trouble, too, is that members of the general public think that Members of Parliament have always had these things free anyway.

The importance of an MP's constituency work lies partly in tangible accomplishments: the pension arrears obtained, the village schoolmistress kept in her job. But it also lies in the links that are forged — or should be — between the ordinary citizens of Britain and those who represent them. The ordinary citizen should feel that there is someone in the system, some identifiable individual, to whom he can turn in case of difficulty and to whom he has a right to expound his views, however untutored. The MP should, for his part, be prevented from losing touch with the thinking and problems of ordinary people. It is often said that constituency work reminds Members of 'where the shoe pinches'.

Our nineteen MPs were conscious of the need to prevent these links from being broken.

You have to learn to deal face to face with constituents at surgeries — learn to shut up, not to try to interrupt the old dear putting her case in her own fashion, to ask where she lives and so on. Let her tell her own story in her own way, long though it may be.

In my constituency there's a perfectly adequate citizens' advice bureau that can deal with everything that I deal with more competently, more expertly, more expeditiously – in every way better. But there are a lot of people who will only talk to me. And they will talk to me because I am the MP and for no other reason.

We're after all talking about the customers at the moment. And I think the customers are entitled to have somebody to come to. They may not know Councillor Smith. They may not know the ward boundaries. But the one thing that most people do know is who their MP is. They know who their MP is, and they come along and they say 'I'm terribly upset' and so on.

The MPs were also aware of the importance of constituency work for preventing them from becoming isolated from the community at large – though many of them insisted, as we have seen, that they are themselves members of the community and therefore unlikely to lose touch completely. Moreover, some Members bear in mind the fact that the people they come into contact with are not all the people.

The people who come to an advice bureau or surgery are not typical of one's constituents at all – any more than the patients who come to a doctor's surgery are typical. They're there because they're untypical, because they need help. One has to remember that.

The trouble is that, when you go to all these functions, as one does, of a non-political nature, you are always approached by the people who feel strongly – by the same sort of people who write to you – not by the great indifferent masses. I try not to pay too much attention to what people say to me or write to me. I still think that, when all is said and done, I've got to use my hunch about what the real feeling is.

The fact that constituency work is so important does, however, pose a dilemma, because even back-bench MPs, as one of them said, do have other things to do; they are members of the national legislature and in many cases potential members of the government. If, on the one hand, they neglect their constituency work or indeed spend anything less than a very large proportion of their time on it, they may be perpetuating individual cases of hardship and injustice and may in a small way be weakening an important link in the chain binding governors to governed. If, on the other, they devote overmuch time and energy to their constituencies, they may fail to inform themselves adequately on matters of national importance and may neglect their central roles as critics of governments and checks on the executive. One of the Labour Members stated the dilemma explicitly:

The MP's constituency work is essential in order to confront him with the realities of life, yes. But the more you involve the Member in dealing with individual cases of this nature, the more you have taken away from his proper function, whether he recognises it or not, which is to be in the House and to pass legislation and to control the executive.

Some MPs manage to resolve the dilemma, or at least to escape from it. One way of responding is to devote oneself almost entirely to the constituency.

That's a fair criticism of people like me. As someone who's got a strong line on the constituency side, I do think that I am, you know, doing a little too much on that. But at my age — I have no ministerial ambitions for one thing — I do feel that, if I'm going to make a mistake, it's going to be in the direction of at least trying to look after the people in my own way.

Another way is not to neglect one's constituency but to give it a relatively low priority.

I'm bound to say I regard constituency work as basically peripheral to my function as a Member of Parliament. I think it is important, but basically it is peripheral. I don't think, frankly, that one is supposed to be a glorified welfare officer to the whole of one's constituency. If one basically believes, as I do, that as an MP one's function is in fact to be a politician in the House of Commons on a national level, then the welfare side of one's life, important though it is, is basically peripheral to that.

But probably most MPs neither resolve the dilemma nor escape from it. They simply live with it, devoting neither as much time to their constituencies as they would like — nor as much to Parliament.

4 Colleagues in the House

In his constituency, the Member of Parliament is unique; there is only one of him. In the House of Commons, by contrast, the MP must work and do business with 629 others, some of his own party, some not. Since no one can accomplish anything entirely on his own, Members must co-operate with others. This chapter and the next are concerned with the organisation provided by the political parties in the House of Commons – and also with the less formal groupings to be found there. Later chapters will go on to deal with the organisation provided, apart from the parties, by Parliament itself: in its rules of procedure, its formally constituted standing committees, and so on.

Members of Parliament do communicate across party lines. They serve on all-party committees, they travel abroad together, they meet informally over meals or in the tea room, they often work together on regional or city problems; sometimes MPs of different parties even have their desks together in the same room. But obviously most friendships in the House, and most political alliances, are formed entirely within one or other of the two great parties. It is to members of his own party that the MP will normally look for advice and support.

Within the parties some of the interchange that goes on is completely informal – random even. An experienced Labour Member disputed the view that MPs talk politics only when they are trying to persuade each other of something:

Influencing isn't done because somebody sits down and says, 'I want to talk to you about X.' There's a continual rub-off of concepts, of ideas. Small pressure groups are temporarily created and do their job or fail to do their job. It happens all the time. It's like one of those modern drawing-room decor things, with the oil that goes up and down inside the water, forming and reforming.

Other MPs also laid stress on the element of casualness:

One factor is where your desk is. If, like me, you are in a room with fifteen others, you are constantly passing them, or they are passing you, and you pass the time of day on politics. If you have bacon and eggs in the canteen two or three times a week, you may sit with the same group of people, and you discuss politics. One very seldom says to oneself, 'I must find Brian.' But if he happens to pass you, you say – well, you know – 'What do you think, mate?'

But by no means all the talk is as casual as this. Some Members make a habit on particular issues of seeking out colleagues they believe to be knowledgeable.

In the field of Northern Ireland – which I'm interested in, and have some knowledge about, but not a lot – I very often talk to one of the Ulster Unionists, or possibly Ian Paisley, to see how they feel about it. They are the people on the spot. I remember, after whatever report it was on the way people were interrogated in Northern Ireland, asking Colin Mitchell [who commanded the Argyll and Sutherland Highlanders in Aden] what his view was.

And over a wide range of issues most MPs are conscious of feeling closer to some of their colleagues than to others, even within the same party.

Some of these 'affinity groups', as one might call them, are fairly well organised, like the Monday Club in the Conservative Party or the Tribune Group on the Labour side. Others are not really groups at all in the organised sense but rather collections of like-minded individuals who tend to view politics in the same sort of way. Two of our Labour MPs were confirmed non-joiners but at the same time did not in any way feel isolated:

Isn't the problem with the Parliamentary Labour Party quite simply this: that there are those on the 'left' and those on the 'right' who are the arch-connivers of politics? They really are. The majority of us, I'm delighted to say, are in the centre, and we don't need to belong to either group because we know that our basic good sense and sanity will show through. It's people like us who elected Ted Short as Deputy Leader [in 1972]. We are a group of like-minded but totally disorganised people.

What I have always felt has been a connection with an amorphous group of people with whom I feel broadly in sympathy. No formal meetings, no discussions, just the occasional sort of word: 'What about so-and-so?' No more than that.

A Conservative also did not belong to any organised group.

But I think that one has people who are sympathetic and are therefore easy to talk to. Broadly they are on the same waveband as you.

Some of those who are joiners, or at least make a practice of consulting their colleagues, do so for reassurance: there is safety in numbers — and emotional security.

I've got a group of friends whom I talk to about lots of things. It's probably a shocking thing to say before my colleagues, but the thing, I think, which does influence me enormously when an issue comes up is this: that, if you are in a group of chaps who are united together, perhaps as a social group, perhaps as an interest group, then your actions are influenced because, if you feel for some reason like changing your mind, you've got this great dread that, if you really do it, you're letting down the boys. It's not so much a question of your opinions, of what you actually think: it's a question of what you do.

Another thing: we come together for protection and reassurance. Take last Wednesday night, for example, when I abstained. I'm sure I would have felt infinitely worse if it had been me sitting on the benches alone. Because there were a whole bunch of us, we didn't feel so bad. It's a terrible thing to say, but I sat there partly because I thought if I didn't they would say I'd gone soft or that the whips had got at me or something like that.

That point about reassurance is very important, particularly if you've got a view that you're a bit uneasy about: you long for someone to say, 'Yes, I agree with you about that.' At least then there are two of you.

That's right. I suppose in the last couple of years I've thought of doing something reasonably distinctive — you know, against the party line — two or three times, and I've sought out two or three people who I thought were sensible, reasonable people to discuss my possible line of action with, before I got myself committed totally.

A minority of MPs are closely associated with one group in the House and only one: the Ulster Unionists to take an obvious example. But most MPs, if they belong to any group at all, belong to several. They have friends in other sections of their party; they talk to different people on different issues. Their circles overlap. In the Labour Party, this is truer now than it was twenty years ago, as one of the older Members pointed out:

On almost any evening you can go into the smoking room, and you can see in Nye Bevan's old corner both the Normans likely — Buchan

and Atkinson – Michael Foot, Harold Lever, Shirley Williams all
talking about the Common Market. The Labour Party at the moment
is leaning over backwards to avoid the factionalism that there was in
the Bevanite/Gaitskellite days of the 'fifties.

Quite possibly, in fact, the Granada dinners could not have
been held on the Labour side twenty years ago.

In the Conservative Party, there have not since the war been
organised factions in the sense of large numbers of Members
acting together in opposition to others over a wide range of
issues.

Take Enoch Powell. I suppose I am slightly on the left wing, if you
can call it a wing, of the Tory party on social matters, and I certainly
am on immigration. Now, having done this anti-Common Market
thing for years and years, I made it quite clear to Enoch, when he
came into the group, that, super, he's on the side of the anti-Market-
eers and we're glad to have him, but so far as I was concerned that
didn't imply that I sympathised with him over all his other things.
Just because we were working together on this one thing, he mustn't
expect me to be one of his cohorts.

I think one is a member of a number of groups. I'm a member of a
group of new Members who would be considered to be left-wing
Tories, and I'm also a member of a group of very strong pro-Mar-
keteers, who in fact cover all the spectrum of the party from fairly
extreme right to fairly extreme left. So one comes across people in
different ways, and different people influence you on different things.

Each party does have one rather exclusive grouping none the
less, apart from the Ulster Unionists: the Monday Club on the
Tory side and the Tribune Group on the Labour. They function similarly.

*Could you say something about how the Monday Club functions in the
House of Commons?*
We have periodic meetings to discuss things and to try to have a
collective view. We don't meet very regularly to be quite frank, not
as regularly as the party committees, but when we do it's usually over
some specific issue. We just have a talk about things, and a general
view emerges, and if you don't follow it there's a certain amount of
feeling.

Most of the Labour Members at the dinners were fascinated to
hear about the Tribune Group. Several of them were also
rather rude about it.

Come on, the secrets of the Tribune Group.

All right, we ought to put the picture straight. We are in the first place the friends of *Tribune* [the weekly left-wing journal]. There is nothing Machiavellian about this: *Tribune* was in need of some parliamentary support. We pay not less than £1 a month by banker's order, and we also contribute to the editorial discussion.

This journalistic fan club is marvellous, but don't kid yourself it has anything to do with the House of Commons.

Well, it does. As far as the Tribune Group is concerned, we have this parliamentary function. On Monday we come together — some of us of similar mind, very much like the Bevanites, come together — to put a point of view. We try and collectively find a way of ...

You mean I can join you for a quid a month?

Sure you can.

Would you put that in writing?

Certainly you can come along. But I don't think you would come there, because why would you want to strengthen the position of people you don't agree with?

I'd come with an open mind.

But, as I was saying, we come together on occasions — unfortunately last year it was not more than three occasions I can think of — for lengthy discussions about the political situation. We try to come to some conclusions as to how far we are getting and what we are doing and so on. In that sense it's purely a discussion group.

But we also ask ourselves how we can maximise our parliamentary influence. And for that purpose we meet much more regularly — on Mondays — in order to secure a collective voice in whatever is happening at the moment — more so possibly in government than in opposition. In this period, in opposition, what we are doing is trying to get a collective view, trying to put to the movement certain ideas, acting as a stimulus, arousing controversy in the sense of discussion about things that we think matter ...

Organising a ticket for the shadow cabinet elections.

Well, strangely enough, you may not believe this ...

No, I don't.

... but as organisers we are less than superb. There are no whips; there are no influences. A vote is never taken at Tribune meetings; there are no votes about things of that sort at all.

The right-wingers at the Labour dinners were even more emphatic that there was no organisation on their side that amounted to anything at all.

It's bloody useless. It's vastly incompetent, both the organisation and the administration. We used to have dinner once a month, which was attended by a very ill-assorted group of people. Talk, that's all it was — all it is, as far as I know.

A map of the informal and unofficial groupings in the House of Commons would be very hard to draw. The Monday Club, the Tribune Group and any organisations which may exist on the Labour right are anxious that not too much should be known about their activities; they want to be able to play down their strength when it suits them — and exaggerate it when it suits them. Many other groups are too inchoate and too volatile to be easy to describe. But alongside these unofficial groups there exists a network of rather more formal meetings and groups organised by the parties. It is not difficult to draw a map of this other network. What needs to be known in its case is how it works and how much influence it has.

The main body on the Conservative side is the 1922 Committee — the '22 for short. (Its proper name is the Conservative Private Members' Committee, but almost no one ever calls it this). The Committee consists of all the Conservative backbenchers including the Ulster Unionists. When the party is in opposition, front-bench spokesmen other than the Leader are welcome to come along; in government, ministers are normally invited to attend only to speak on their own subjects. The Committee may meet at other times, but its regular meeting is at 6 o'clock on Thursday evenings. The Committee does not go in for formal debates — there are no resolutions or votes — but whips are always there to make sure that ministers and the party leaders know what has gone on.

Several of the Conservatives at the dinners were not inclined to take the full meetings of the Committee very seriously.

There is one great drawback the '22 Committee has, and that is that there are one or two people who leave the meeting and pick up a telephone and ring up a newspaper. So, if you're going to say something fairly pungent and critical, you would no more say it at the 1922 Committee than you would fly out of this window — because I am not prepared to hurt my party by speaking out at a meeting that is theoretically supposed to be confidential but isn't.
But you do go all the same.
Yes, I go. I go along to find out a bit in advance what's happening next week. But the point about how un-private it is is absolutely

right. A lot of people, including me, never speak – and certain people, who may not talk very much elsewhere, tend to have rather a lot to say there.

How many of you go along to the meetings?
I go about as often as I go to Ascot. [*Laughter*].
I don't attend very regularly, not because I've any hard feelings about it, but because, having attended it before, I honestly didn't think it was the best way of spending one's time.

Surprisingly enough, almost the only Member prepared to defend the full meetings as being at least potentially useful was the one who attended about as often as he went to Ascot. He said, in effect, that they could be important as a safety valve.

Could we put it negatively? The '22 ensures that no great feeling could well up within the party during the week that would not find expression, if it was a great feeling, on the Thursday night that the '22 meets. Now in a negative sense that is an important mechanism. It may not happen very often, but the weekly meetings make it certain that nothing could build up to a point where the Prime Minister and the Government were blasted out of office. It would find expression at the regular meeting: I've never yet known anyone with such a deep-laid plot that he couldn't resist blasting off at the '22.

But, if the full meetings are important really only as a safety valve, the regular meetings of the Committee's officers and its Executive are, it would seem, another matter. The Committee has six officers (chairman, vice-chairmen and so on) and an Executive of twelve who meet together at least once a week, usually before the full meeting. The MPs at the dinners were clear that the officers and the Executive between them were a major channel of communication between backbenchers and leaders. Among those present were an officer and a member of the Executive.

How far do you regard yourselves as, in effect, the leaders of a back-bench pressure group vis-à-vis the Government?
'Pressure group' is too strong a term. The thing is that I don't regard myself as anything other than just a single chap, who is in the House of Commons a lot and who mixes. And if anything comes to me – I don't necessarily go and seek it, but you get a feeling, a smell – then I bring it up. I wouldn't put it any higher than that. But, if you get fourteen people (or whatever it is) doing that, or maybe twelve out of

the fourteen, and it all fits into a pattern, that's a sort of red light.
And then you actually regard it as your duty to warn the Government ...
Oh yes, if I got a smell of something and mentioned it, and then
others, quite independently, said, 'Well, yes, I've got the same feeling', then I think the chairman would rightly say, 'This is an important thing, we must investigate it.' And wider consultations would
take place and, if then it was confirmed, I think he would go and see
the Prime Minister and tell him. Would that be right?

Yes. And there have been two meetings within the last ten years that
have been absolutely vital. I go to most of the meetings, and they're
always interesting and intermittently important. But on these two
occasions they were absolutely vital.

The Members present were reluctant to say which the two had
been, but they clearly concerned the party leadership.
    One of those who was sure that the full meetings of the '22
do not much matter called attention to the importance of the
specialist party committees on the Conservative side.

If you want an open debate which is really important and influences
Cabinet, then you go to one of the party committees – Foreign
Affairs, Home, or whatever – and that's where people really let fly
and that's what matters.

At the time of the dinners, there were nineteen such committees on the Conservative side, each of them corresponding
more or less to one of the major government departments. The
chairman and officers when the Conservatives are in power are
all backbenchers and, as in the case of the 1922 Committee,
ministers attend by invitation. Although the committees have
officers, they have no fixed membership and any Member can
attend any meeting he wants to. On an important occasion,
nearly a hundred MPs will suddenly turn up to a committee
usually attended by only ten or a dozen regulars.
    One of the attractions of party committees is that they are
much more likely than debates in the House to give Members
a chance to air their views.

You have to remember that MPs do like to talk in some sort of
organised framework. Now, however energetic you are, you can only
talk on the floor of the House, at most, every two or three weeks; and
therefore, there you are, you want to say something, you think it's
important, so you go up to the committee, and you're bound really to

be called because people only talk for about two minutes. For those who are energetic this is the most suitable forum.

They are also attractive because backbenchers believe them to be influential.

There's no need to be mysterious about this. A whip is allocated to every committee. He sits there taking notes. If that committee is clearly going in a particular direction or a row is brewing, a report is in the hands of the Chief Whip within five minutes of the end of that committee. And I've sat on several committees in recent months where I'm perfectly clear the Chief Whip has been got to not in five minutes but in one. And this is where we start changing views, because that whip will go back to the Chief Whip and say, 'We've had a very ugly meeting up here — eighty present — and the view was taken that ...' So there's no mystery: if a committee really blows off steam, it's in Cabinet the next day.

Sheer numbers are clearly important. An attendance of eighty at a meeting, if it were on a controversial subject, would be bound to shake any Chief Whip. So is the type of matter under discussion. Backbenchers are not likely to be able to exert much influence in such technical fields as (to take the extreme case) defence: they are more likely to be influential in fields where emotion plays a part and where one man's opinion is thought to be as good as another's.

Home Affairs and Northern Ireland both fall into that category at the moment, and quite important influences can suddenly be felt and made to register. It is very difficult to start arguing about types of ships or about types of aircraft. But Northern Ireland and the Home Office are to an extent emotional, instinctual. It's the instinctual things that come out of these committees that count.

According to the Members at the dinners, the committees also gain influence from the fact that, although they are generally at their weakest in matters involving a high degree of expertise and technical knowledge, the Conservative Parliamentary Party does contain a fairly large number of acknowledged experts, especially in the fields of commerce and finance.

I always think the most interesting example of this is when the Chancellor of the Exchequer has made his Budget speech and the Opposition has replied. Within ten minutes of the Opposition spokesman sitting down, the Finance Committee meets and the Chancellor comes to elaborate what he has said. Practically the whole party turns up to this meeting and, whatever subject he has dealt with in his tax reforms or whatever it is, there's always some chap who gets up and who happens to be an expert on that thing. I remember there was something to do with building: up jumps Albert Costain who is in fact a builder. Something to do with finance, and up jumps Harry D'Avigdor-Goldsmid, who is a bullion broker. No one of these people may know more than five per cent of the area, but amongst them all they cover the ground. It's impressive.

In fields apart from commerce and finance, many of the committees have Members on them who are either active in particular lines of business or else make a point of keeping in touch with particular professions or industries.

In aviation at the moment we're rather lucky because most of the officers — I think all of them — have in fact had something to do with the aircraft industry. Therefore we can offer something to the Minister.

Shipbuilding's a good example. We've got one or two experts on shipbuilding, and the point is that, when you have three or four people who keep constantly in touch with the Chamber of Shipping and the shipbuilding employers, when an issue does come up, we know who to go to — who to get the facts from.

In the nature of the case, concrete examples of the committees' influence are hard to come by, but our MPs could offer at least two they were quite clear about.

The classic case, of course, is the creation of Granada — of independent television. This was almost entirely due to a combination of the 1922 Committee and the back-bench Broadcasting Committee. It's perfectly plain that the Government of the time didn't want to break the BBC's television monopoly. And it's equally plain that after one rather magical meeting of the 1922 Committee, which was followed by meetings of the Broadcasting Committee, the Government changed their mind.

Another Member could think of a more recent example.

I won't specify when it was, but there was a very, very full meeting on the subject of Northern Ireland, when it was made perfectly clear that the soldiers were having their hands tied behind their backs. And there was a hell of a row. Some of us who were in Northern Ireland shortly afterwards learned that the appropriate directive had been altered with effect from that date. That in itself did not prove that the Committee had done it. What was conclusive was the number of people in the Government who came to us subsequently and said, 'Lest you be under any illusion, I wouldn't like you to think that that meeting had any effect whatever on our policy in Northern Ireland, because our policy remains absolutely unchanged.' Unchanged my foot.

If the committees are important as, at the very least, possible focuses for back-bench discontent, it is not surprising that Conservative ministers try to remain on good terms with them and indeed to nobble them. A Member active in party committee work emphasised the importance of their retaining their independence.

Ministers are always anxious to be on excellent terms with the officers of the committee affecting their department. And they will, as far as they can, and this is interesting, seek to take you into their confidence. Now, ministers taking committee participants into their confidence is like ministers taking journalists into their confidence: once the confidences have been exchanged, you are to an extent inhibited. My own feeling is that the officers of a committee need to keep a certain distance: you must not allow ministers to emasculate your performance by letting them tell you too much of what they propose to do. You mustn't feel in any sense that you're part of – an agency of – the Government.

The role played by back-bench bodies is bound to vary depending on whether a party is in government or not; and, to make this part of the Labour discussion more comparable to the Conservatives', the Labour MPs were asked mainly to recall the time when they were in power before 1970. Superficially, Labour's organisation in the House resembles the Conservatives' fairly closely. There is a weekly meeting of the Parliamentary Labour Party (PLP), roughly equivalent to the 1922 Committee, and there are 'subject groups', more or less equivalent to the Conservatives' party committees. The PLP, however, operates on a quite different basis from the 1922 Committee. All Labour MPs, including ministers and front-bench spokesmen, are full members, and resolutions are frequently moved and votes taken. In opposition at least, the views of the PLP majority are supposed to be binding on the

party in the House. The PLP thus has considerably more status than the 1922 Committee, at least in form.

This being so, it is perhaps surprising that the Labour MPs
did not seem to have thought very much about the PLP's role.
Most of the Conservatives seemed to have asked themselves
whether the 1922 Committee had influence and, if so, why; the
Labour Members seemed to take the PLP very much for
granted. There was agreement, however, that on some subjects
backbenchers had exerted some influence on the Labour Government. It was an ex-minister who said:

Leaving aside the business of the actual votes, I would have thought
that the long, steady, back-breaking work of Bob Sheldon and Joel
Barnett on East of Suez had a big impact via the Parliamentary
Labour Party. I would say that it was the existence of the PLP and
the fight about prices and incomes policy which began to modify
Government attitudes, leading up to the great crises [in June 1969]
over *In Place of Strife*. On *In Place of Strife*, I think it's just possible – I'm not sure about this, but it's just possible – that the Government might have taken on the unions on that; but it was made so
demonstrably clear at successive party meetings that on this one they
would be sunk if they did that the Cabinet were led to change their
minds.

Going back to the question of votes, it's the vote in the House that
really matters and the thing about the PLP is that it can warn the
Government in advance – prevent the Government from doing anything suicidal. And the Government can get a pretty clear warning
without actually being defeated at the meeting. And, in situations
that are not crisis situations, continual pressure on the Government – if I can use East of Suez as an example – can change opinion,
can be effective.

It may be that Labour Members are inclined to attribute less
influence to the PLP than Tories do to the 1922 Committee
because the PLP actually is less influential. But it seems more
probable that the sense of disenchantment on the Labour side
results simply from the fact that Labour MPs want more and
expect more. A degree of influence that would seem to Conservatives quite considerable seems to Labour Members hardly worth having. No one stated this view explicitly at the dinners, but the remarks of one Member were at least consistent
with it.

The fact is that Parliament, the PLP and all the rest of it function only after a decision's been taken. There's all this secrecy, there are inspired leaks, there's the whole paraphernalia of government. The decision is taken at the top of the mountain; it slides down the side of the mountain into the laps of those waiting in the Parliamentary Labour Party; and you've then got to discuss the thing with the decision taken and publicly known.

So therefore, in a period of Labour Government, the PLP finds itself in the curious situation of having perpetually to give the Government a vote of confidence or no confidence – after the decision has come down the mountain. What this leads to is hole-in-the-corner, subversive meetings with ministers, trying to get influence, trying to talk into the ears of people with some influence, and so on.

It is striking that the Conservatives, although they might have winced at some of this Member's language ('hole-in-the-corner', 'subversive'), would have thought that such private meetings between backbenchers and ministers, far from being somehow disreputable, were precisely what was required.

When Labour is in power more than a hundred votes at PLP meetings – nearly one-third of the total, sometimes more – are cast by ministers and parliamentary private secretaries ('bag carriers' as one of the MPs insisted on calling them). This pay-roll vote makes it virtually impossible for the party leaders to be defeated: for a critical motion to be carried, the backbenchers would have to vote for it by a margin of three or four to one.

If there's one thing that distresses me most about the Labour Party, it's the activities of the PLP. Take something very dear to my heart: health charges. What happens? We're discussing teeth and spectacles charges. The only bugger who wants them is ——— and the rest of the Cabinet should have ... but that's another question. So they have a PLP about it. And about half-past twelve the room suddenly fills up. Magical. Where have they come from? They've come from all over the place – the pay-roll vote, the best part of a hundred votes. It's a disgrace.

At the Conservative dinners, as we saw, considerable stress was laid on the importance of the specialist party committees. The Labour dinners confirmed what most people suspected already: that the comparable Labour 'subject groups' are far less important. One Member did speak up for them –

they can be very useful for backbenchers because, since they're better informed than the PLP as a whole, they can force the front-bench spokesman to accommodate himself to their views.

— but most of the others admitted rather sadly that they do not have much weight.

How many of you actually go to subject groups?
The answer is very, very few, whether it's around this table or throughout the PLP. Very, very few.

One of the worst attended groups in my experience — and I'm as guilty as anyone else on this — is Social Security about which we ought to feel strongly. I once went quite regularly but ... [*he shrugged his shoulders*].

My record on subject groups is as appalling as the vast majority of my colleagues. I just don't go.

The one major exception to this general rule is the Trade Union Group, but the Trade Union Group is not strictly a subject group and owes its standing primarily to its being the parliamentary expression of Labour's close ties with the unions.

Part of the explanation for the subject groups' weakness may also be part of the explanation for the Labour Members' apparent lack of interest — as compared with the Conservatives — in all of their various back-bench organisations. On the Conservative side, policy is made almost entirely by Conservatives in Parliament, including the party leadership. In the Labour Party, policy is made partly by the PLP and its leaders but partly also by extra-parliamentary bodies like the National Executive Committee and annual conference. Many backbenchers who are experts on particular subjects are now members, or potential members, of NEC committees and tend to regard this link as more important than their link, if any, with the appropriate subject group. Even when Labour is in government, MPs seeking to exert an influence may choose to operate through extra-parliamentary channels.

Another factor that may be in play is that, since Labour backbenchers are reluctant to make a sharp hierarchical distinction between themselves and their leaders (or ministers in a Labour Government), they may also be reluctant to become, as it were, 'professional' back-bench MPs. Conservative Members accept an element of hierarchy — or at least of division of labour — in their party and are prepared to form exclusively back-bench bodies which have as their purpose the putting of a specifically back-bench point of view. Labour Members appear unwilling to accept the sharp distinctions of status that such procedures imply.

This chapter has dealt with, amongst other things, aspects of parliamentary life in which the two political parties differ significantly. The next chapter deals with an aspect in which the parties' differences, although they exist, are far outweighed by their similarities: the role of the whips in enforcing party discipline.

5 The Whips

The discipline of Britain's parliamentary parties has declined quite rapidly in recent years. Back-bench revolts in the House of Commons — taking the form of declared abstentions or even of voting with the other side — are much more common now than they were in the 'forties or 'fifties. The Granada dinners were held shortly after the passage through the Commons of the European Communities Bill, during which there were repeated rebellions by minorities on both sides. And on the night of one of the dinners the Government was defeated by thirty-five votes on the introduction of a new set of immigration rules. In fact the dinner ended when it was learned that the vote in the House was due in the next half-hour.

Nevertheless, by the standards of other countries — even including those with parliamentary systems modelled on the British — the level of party cohesion in this country is high. In the great majority of divisions, every Conservative MP present votes in one lobby and every Labour MP in the other. The explanations for this high level of cohesion are various. Government backbenchers wish to maintain the Government in power, Opposition Members, if they can, to defeat it. MPs of both parties are reluctant to appear disunited in public, believing that the electorate will penalise a disunited party at the polls. Britain, moreover, is a relatively homogeneous country, lacking the sorts of deep regional divisions that undermine party unity in other countries. Discipline in the House of Commons is reinforced by the sanctions which, as we have already seen, are available to local parties and associations: votes of censure, reprimands and ultimately the refusal to readopt. Finally, MPs of the same party tend to vote together simply because they tend to agree with one another; they would probably not be in the same party if they did not.

Against this background, the party whips in the House have three main tasks. The first is purely organisational and consists of ensuring that MPs know when to vote and which way their party wants them to vote. This task has nothing to do with discipline and would have to be performed even if all Members of either party always wanted to vote the same way. The second task is the disciplinary one: trying to persuade Members who do not want to vote with their party that they have a duty to, or that it is in their interest to. The third task arises directly out of the second. It consists of conveying the views of the party leaders to backbenchers and more particularly, as we saw in the last chapter, of warning the leaders of back-bench discontent. These last two tasks – not the purely organisational one – were the ones discussed at the dinners.

Although they were not invited on this basis, the nineteen MPs who attended the dinners turned out to be a fairly rebellious lot. Fifteen had rebelled against their party at one time or another, some of them many times. Several of the Conservatives told stories about the revolt on the Government's immigration rules that had taken place only the week before.

You voted with the Opposition. Is that right?
Yes. Well, not quite: I voted against the proposal before the House.
Did the whips make any attempt to stop you?
No, no. I'll tell you what they did. I was lunching with a friend, who shall be anonymous, in the City, and also with a colleague, a Member of Parliament, in my friend's office. We were sitting round the boardroom table, just like this. We'd finished the smoked salmon and were onto the chicken, and the phone rang. Our host answered it, and it was the Chief Whip for my parliamentary colleague. He'd heard that this chap might be abstaining and he – the Chief Whip himself – tried to talk him out of it. Then my colleague said, 'Do you know that —— is here?' 'Oh, that's all right,' Francis [Pym] said, 'We know about him.' And no attempt was made to get me to change my mind because I'd made it very clear what I was going to do.

What about you? You abstained. Did the whips try to influence you?
No. I simply told my whip, and he said to me, very kindly, 'I've told the Chief Whip we must never approach you because you make up your mind and, if we do approach you, it can make things worse.' So I told him, 'I think there's going to be a massive abstention tonight, and I strongly recommend that Carr [the Home Secretary] say in his speech that he's going to take back the rules pending discussions with the Commonwealth prime ministers. If you do, I think you'll get through later on.' And he said, 'Yes, I think you're right.' He said they were having a meeting of the whips that night, and he would put forward that point of view. He certainly made no attempt to influence my decision.

The failure of the whips to exert pressure on that occasion, when the Government was actually defeated, is remarkable enough. Perhaps even more remarkable is how little pressure the whips on both sides seem to have put on Members over a much more important issue: the Common Market. Not one of the Labour MPs who rebelled in the critical division on 28 October 1971 reported that the whips had threatened them in any way beforehand or tried to punish them in any way afterwards.

I had intended to vote for entry; in the event, I abstained. But this had nothing whatever to do with the whips, who in fact said almost nothing to me at all on this. My regional whip would see me in the tea room and say he was slightly worried and ask me what I was going to do — that sort of thing. But there was certainly no pressure. No, I decided to abstain rather than vote with the Tories because, as I said once before, I did not want to go against some of my most reliable and trusted friends in the constituency.

All that happened to me was that a whip would come up and say, 'Are you still going to vote in favour?' And I would say 'Yes', and he would say 'OK' and go away.

What could the whips do? I would love to be able to say that I deliberately put my career on the line. I would love to be able to say that; but it wouldn't be true. My constituency party is pro-Market. My trade union, oddly enough, is pro-Market. What the hell can Mellish [the Labour Chief Whip] do with me? He can't tell my constituency party to get rid of me: they agree with me. What can he do?

Not only was there virtually no pressure on the Labour side; there appears to have been very little on the Tory either, even though it was the centre-piece of the Government's entire policy that was at stake. A prominent anti-Marketeer said there was some pressure:

because before the vote in October chaps were wheeled up to Ted Heath — quite a few of them — and Ted Heath talked to them. I suppose that was pressure but there was not much to it.

A Conservative Member who rebelled consistently on the Bill remarked:

It might interest you to know that, with all the times on the Common Market I didn't do what they wanted me to, never once did any whip try to persuade me to do otherwise. It's rather interesting.

Nor, apart from the meetings with the Prime Minister, were any serious cases of pressure reported in the press at the time.

Almost all of our MPs were emphatic that the whips do not – contrary to what is commonly believed – go in for arm-twisting. Not on the Common Market, not on anything else.

On Northern Ireland at some stages it was a question either of voting against the party or abstaining. The whips said, 'If you think the Government is bound to fail, you must vote against; but if you think they should be given the benefit of the doubt, then you should abstain.' And I abstained. [*Was that the total conversation?*] That was the total conversation.

Yes, I was once asked to give them the benefit of the doubt. It was after a dinner. A great friend of mine who's a whip – a really charming man – asked me what I was unhappy about, and then said, 'Well, wouldn't you abstain?' So I did. But what it was on I can't remember.

I call them not so much whips as feather dusters.

The main reason why the whips do not go in much for exerting pressure is that they have very little to press with. In the words of the MP quoted earlier: 'What *can* they do?' They cannot prevent a Member attending the House, they cannot prevent him from voting or visiting his constituency, they cannot prevent him from being readopted at the next election: 'As long as my local party is satisfied with me, none of them – not Mellish, not Wilson, not Transport House – can do very much about it.' The whips can of course shout, but this will disturb only the minority of MPs who mind being shouted at. One of our Labour Members evidently rather enjoyed it.

There was one famous occasion just after Bob Mellish had been appointed Chief Whip. The idea was that Wilson had appointed him to straighten us all out; the party had been unruly and he was going to restore some order. A lot of nonsense, but anyway ... I'd done something I shouldn't have done. And Mellish – the hard man of British politics, who'd come in to straighten us out – fetched me in, and in front of all the whips in the office – they were very sceptical about what was coming to them – launched a tirade against me. Against me personally. And it went on and on, and then suddenly he made the fatal tactical error of stopping for breath. And in the split second that was available to me I looked him straight in the eye and said, 'Come on, give us a kiss.' And the place erupted with laughter, and Bob Mellish and I have been great friends ever since. I've never been disciplined, never been threatened with anything.

The whips can always plead with Members not to damage the Government or the party; but, even when they do, their main weapon is still the power of reason. Two of the MPs at the dinners described cases where there had been long discussions. In one case the Member had been talked out of rebelling, in the other not. But in both the main weapon used – indeed the only weapon used – was rational argument.

What happened – this was very early on in the time of the Labour Government – was that the House of Lords in its judicial capacity had issued a judgement in favour of the Burmah Oil Company: on a point of compensation, which arose out of the decision to burn the oilfields in Burma at the time of the Japanese invasion. The Government then introduced a bill with the intention, retrospectively, of reversing the Lords' decision.

I remember this was something which a lot of us who were lawyers felt was not right. I remember writing to the Lord Chancellor, and then being seen by the Attorney-General and by one of the Treasury ministers, who was in charge of the bill. I'm bound to say that the whips didn't put any sort of pressure on me, in terms of any sort of sanction. But I was convinced by the ministers that the bill was right, despite my earlier view, and in the end I spoke in all the stages of it.

It is significant that in this case the power of reason was deployed, not mainly by the whips, but by ministers – that is, by those who, because they had a grasp of the details of the measure, were in the best position to deploy it.

In the other case, by contrast, the only people who spoke to the Member, a Conservative, were the whips – probably because the arguments to be used were purely tactical. The incident occurred while the Conservatives were still in opposition.

Basically what happened was that I told my own whip what my views were. He made a mild attempt to talk me out of it. Then two other whips came, and they had a go at me, but very mildly, and then they asked that I go and discuss it with Willie Whitelaw, who was still the Chief Whip then.

I went, and we had a long talk. There certainly were no threats or
blandishments used. As I recall, Willie's main approach to me was,
first of all, to find out whether I had really thought through my own
position; and, when he discovered that I had thought it through and
was absolutely convinced, his main appeal was on the basis that he
had a very difficult job keeping the Tory Party together on the issue
and of containing extremists on the other side and that, if I went
along with the leadership on this one, I would find that everything
would be all right. But I was not entirely persuaded and finally I
abstained.

Although the whips seldom exert pressure in any overt way,
Members may suffer all the same as a consequence of rebelling. At one of the Conservative dinners, considerable discussion developed about whether there is a price to be paid for
rebellion and, if so, what form the price takes. The Members
present disagreed about how the whips actually behave. They
also differed in their own sensitivity to different kinds of considerations (what is a heavy price to one man may hardly be
noticed by another). The discussion was opened by someone
who does rebel fairly often.

I've never been in any 'trouble' in the strict sense; but you do know,
when you vote against the party on something that embarrasses it,
that there are disciplines operating which are not apparent. For example, if you are known as a troublemaker, you know that your
chances of getting a job – a job in the Government – will be less.
You know that your chance, perhaps, of getting an MBE for one of
your hard-working constituency officers will be less. Perhaps your
own chance of getting to the House of Lords when the time comes.
Now you do think of these things. They do weigh with you.

I have some reservations about the thing about the MBE. I know it
does go on, but I'm in no position to accuse the whips of dirty work
at the crossroads. I don't know how far individual sanctions are ap-
plied to those to whom they may speak smooth words, or not speak
at all, but whom they afterwards mark down as not to be promoted
or to be punished in some petty way. My instinct is that they don't
do it because ultimately it would catch up with them and spoil a
system that they are anxious to show is fair.

You may well be right, but what ——— says about MBEs and so on
goes on in his mind goes on in mine too. But, even if it does, you
can't say to yourself, 'I'm not going to do something because if I do I

won't ever be in the Government or get to the House of Lords or whatever.' If that were the line, then to hell with it.

I'm amazed at some of this. It would never enter my head – the question of honours for people, the House of Lords, all that – it would never enter my head. The whole system of honours and Buckingham Palace garden parties leaves me, and I think most of the younger Members, entirely cold.

It depends on what the whips think is going on. You see the whips do, I think, distinguish between the man who from time to time puts his foot down and says no, and the man who is a constant nuisance for motives which the whips suspect to be personal and possibly rather selfish. Now I would expect the second category not to find great favour. If there were three men to be chosen for an overseas trip, I think the whips might just decide that he would not be one of the three. I think with the constant nuisance that could well arise. But I think it is nonsense to think that the man who follows his conscience from time to time gets a discreditable mark.

No strictly comparable discussion took place at the Labour dinners but, if one had, the division of opinion would probably have been very similar (though without the same concern for MBEs). One or two of the Labour rebels were not at all dismayed by the consequences of their experience.

I've paid some price in terms of isolation within the party, but on the other hand the line I've taken has been very good for my standing in the constituency.

Yes, one's felt isolated, but that's because of the merits of the case. You can't rebel on a three-line whip against your own party and expect everybody to receive you with open arms the day after.

Only one rebel on the Labour side was very conscious of what his indiscipline may have cost him.

I got the message early on, very soon after I got elected in fact. There was some question of offences against the code of conduct, and for some unaccountable reason I was hailed before a four-man committee – Herbert Bowden, who'd been Chief Whip and was then Leader of the House; Ted Short, the Chief Whip; and Manny Shinwell, who was Chairman of the parliamentary party – and one other, I think, Willie Hamilton, one of the vice-chairmen. The interview went on about my offences, and at the end of the meeting it was agreed that Short and Manny Shinwell should give me some advice.

The advice was that Members should behave themselves, particularly younger Members, because they had their whole future in front of them. Life in Parliament, they said, could be enjoyable. There are foreign visits which are pleasant – it's an opportunity to meet and see people throughout the world, and to do so in comfort – and there are various other things that go in recognition of good behaviour. The Whips' Office puts in nominations to a lot of things. They obviously have a list of people, of elevated Members, who get various perks: the goodies of parliamentary life. And you can get exonerated from the arduous tasks. And this is really the basis of discipline.

The Member in question said he did not mind being excluded from all these things ('I don't travel very well so I'm not falling over myself to be included, but I've never been delegated to cross Parliament Square'). But he had been excluded all the same. And there was never any question of his entering the Government.

Members defy their parties for all sorts of reasons. They may be under pressure from their constituents, they may feel strongly about a particular subject, they may just enjoy rebelling. Whatever their motives, rebels usually claim that their main aim is to influence the Government or the party leadership.

As Members of Parliament we do not actually make decisions ourselves, but we try to influence them. The whole point of threatening to withhold one's vote is to get things moved a bit.

That's it, absolutely. If your party's in government, what you aim to hear in your mind's ear is the Chief Whip saying to the Prime Minister: 'Now, Prime Minister, we've got this coming up at Cabinet next week. I think I ought to warn you that I've had eight or ten letters about it, and I think the colleagues ought to know that feeling in the party is such and such.' Now let's say that this is at the heart of the decision before the Cabinet. The Chief Whip attends every Cabinet, and the Prime Minister will say, 'Chief Whip, have you anything to tell us?' And the Chief Whip says, 'Yes, I'm bound to tell you that I've had some letters from people I know are not speaking just for themselves.' And that is the decisive moment.

The question arose at both series of dinners of how this sort of influence can best be exerted. All of the Conservatives and most of the Labour Members were sure that, if backbenchers really do want to make an impact on their leaders, they must notify the whips well in advance of any action they propose to take. Instant rebellion is pointless.

The whole essence of any serious intention to rebel is to give plenty of notice so that you can be sure of getting a chance to put your view. In the end, a vote against your leaders is an admission that you've failed to move them on something — is an admission of defeat.

Most of us know when issues are coming up. One can think far enough ahead and give notice. I did just this on a particular issue recently. Thinking about it during the latter part of the summer and over my holiday, I decided that I could not bring myself to vote with the Government on this matter again. I didn't know whether there was going to be a three-line whip or anything like that, but what I did know was that it would be appropriate to give notice in the proper way. So I wrote to a certain party and said, 'Look, I'm sorry but I must tell you this. I can't bring myself to do this again.' That was longish notice, but I thought, 'Well, the longer you know about this beforehand the better.'

The one absolutely unforgivable thing is to come in at the end of a debate on a subject in which one is not particularly interested and to hear the Opposition rejoinder — from somebody who has perhaps got some rather better phrases for his case than the Government has — and, as a result of that, to walk into the lobby against the Government. That is just not tolerable and on the whole is just not done.

It also matters who the rebels are. The few persistent rebels at the dinners were not inclined to say so, but most of the others present were quite clear that, other things being equal, the more loyal someone has been prior to threatening to rebel, the better the chances of his rebellion's having some effect. The Member who makes a habit of rebelling, unless he is unexpectedly joined by others, can be ignored — and usually is.

If you get somebody like Enoch Powell, I really don't think the Government pay any attention to what his action is likely to be on anything, because he's very much on his own on almost everything. I would have thought there is a great difference between him and some like ———— who's taken up an issue like the Market but doesn't make a habit of rebelling on everything else as well.

Going back to what we hope is being discussed in Cabinet, they say,

'Well, X, Y and Z have all said that they're going to do something. But they're old hands: we know their line: they're out to knock the Government. But on the other hand A, B and C have also said that they're going to do the same thing, and they're newcomers to this game, and therefore we really ought to weigh this rather carefully.'

One of the Labour Members was sure that what shook the Labour Government on its proposed Industrial Relations Bill in 1969 was precisely this reinforcement of the predictable rebels by the unpredictable.

I found that, when a normal supporter of the Government like me had doubts and reservations, it had an effect — not because one individual was involved but because he represented a band of opinion in the party, on whom the Government had normally been able to rely.

Most of the MPs believed that rebellions and threats of rebellion could influence policy, perhaps usually only at the margins, but sometimes, as with the Labour Government's aborted Industrial Relations Bill, on a major issue. Only one or two were totally sceptical. One younger Conservative complained quite bitterly that, when rebellions occurred, it did not mean that backbenchers were being listened to; it meant precisely that they were not.

I'm not claiming great wisdom. I may be the biggest idiot who ever set foot under the sun. But I am an elected Member of Parliament and I am a member of the Conservative Party, and I do think I have a right to feel that something of what I say is listened to. It may be dismissed after having been considered as not having any great weight. But three hundred of us do have a right to have a voice and, if we aren't listened to, we will show our frustration in the only way we can: in the lobbies.

A Labour Member similarly shook his head, rather cynically.

On the Land Commission, which nobody was very interested in except me, I flouted three-line whips throughout. I was rather hoping each time that the Chief Whip of the day or the Prime Minister would call me in to threaten to discipline me, so that I could tell them exactly what was wrong with the Land Commission. The trouble was, they ignored me completely. And every revolt I've ever been involved in has been absolutely and totally ignored.

This Member's view was that, while there is hardly any discipline in the Labour Party at the moment, there is hardly any back-bench influence either. But this view was a minority one.

A backbencher seeking to influence policy can, as we have seen, make use of party organisations like the 1922 Committee, the Parliamentary Labour Party or the two parties' specialist committees. He can make representations via the party whips. He can threaten to rebel against the party. But he can also try to make his influence felt not so much via his party as in the House of Commons itself: either on the floor or in committee. It was to the Member of Parliament in his central role as member of the national legislature that we turned next.

6 All-Rounders and Specialists

We remarked at the end of Chapter 1 that there are as many ways of being an MP as there are MPs. To be sure, Members are constrained in a variety of ways: they cannot flout the rules of the House with impunity; they cannot avoid doing at least a certain minimal amount of work in the constituency. None the less, Members of Parliament are to a remarkable degree free to be what they choose to be. They can, within limits, be idle or industrious, constituency-centred or Westminster-centred, silent or outspoken, specialists or generalists. This chapter deals with some of the choices individual MPs have to make, and also with how Members prepare themselves to take part in parliamentary discussion and debate.

There was a large measure of consensus at the dinners about the qualities an MP must exhibit if he is to impress his colleagues. For one thing, he must actually attend the House. As a Conservative put it:

Whatever else you may say about Enoch Powell, he's in the House of Commons more than a lot of people. I'm often in a debate or even at question time when I suddenly say to myself, 'I wonder if Enoch's around.' And I look up and by gum he's there. The first bit of advice you would give to any new Member is that, if you're going to make an impression in the House, you must be seen occasionally to be there.

To be there and to speak. But not too often.

I'm just thinking of Emrys Hughes's advice to a new Member. 'Look, Emrys,' the new man said, 'you're long in the tooth. You've been here a long time. I spoke on the day of the Queen's Speech, I've made numerous interventions since, put down dozens of questions, I've made another six speeches. What more can I do?' Emrys said, 'Go back home and stay there for the rest of the session.'

And the Member, especially the new Member, should not be a publicity-seeker.

One admires the man who can capture a headline, not for himself, but for the point of view he's trying to put forward. But, if one thinks that he's merely doing things to get his own name in the headlines, this does not impress.

But it is not enough for an MP to be about the place, and not actually to alienate his colleagues. He has to exhibit some positive qualities.

The great thing in the House of Commons is that you've got to be listened to. If people aren't prepared to listen to you, even if they disagree with you, then you're dead. The most important quality that backbenchers — or frontbenchers for that matter — have to have, first of all, is the capacity to articulate their views. Otherwise the thing doesn't get off the ground at all.

Secondly, they have to have some knowledge of what it is they're supposed to be talking about. Thirdly and perhaps most importantly, the House of Commons will on the whole wear the most extraordinary views provided they believe that the individual expressing them actually believes what he is saying. The man who does worst is the chap who gets up on every single occasion, on every different subject, and makes a speech which he thinks will go down well with his own side or, if he's a member of some rebel group, with his own group. Nobody believes a bloody word he says, and he'll be dead within eighteen months.

You don't win respect only by making speeches. You've got to give some indication of work, of doing some research, of knowing what you're talking about.

I can think of a number of Members who are listened to with keen interest and, if not admiration, at least respect, because they are patently sincere and because they've done their homework. And it's amazing, you are often listening to a Member who is not at all a good speaker and you are thinking, 'Well, this is a fair point he's making.'

Finally, it is important, though by no means universal, for Members to speak with authority — preferably with the authority that stems either from first-hand experience or from a legitimate claim to speak on behalf of some interest or group outside.

One curious thing about the House is the very small number of people of whom you can say, when they are speaking, that they are speaking for anybody but themselves. Ian Paisley was an exception. When he first came into the House, he was listened to in a very special way because he really did speak for something in Northern Ireland. He wasn't just speaking as someone who happened to get elected because he'd been selected by his party.

The House likes to hear the trade union Member who speaks from recent experience. They're not really interested in a trade unionist who hasn't been to a branch meeting for twenty years. They're quite interested to hear the industrial manager, business man, banker even, who can speak with authority about lending rates or about management from the management side of industry. I have outside interests of my own — they're well known — and the House doesn't seem to mind that if they feel it helps you make a better contribution.

There was general agreement that someone seeking to make an impact in the House should know what he is talking about. But there was much less agreement about whether he should try to become, in any strict sense, a specialist. Should Members try to master one or two subjects, make them their own? Or should they give some thought to, and be prepared to speak on, the whole range of current politics? Pressures to specialise are certainly felt.

You almost have to specialise today. There is so much legislation going through, and one can be lost if one is just a fielder and not a batsman, to use a cricketing term.

The selection of speakers for debates has this effect too. I've just put in a letter, before coming here, asking to be called in the debate tomorrow. And I pointed out in my letter, as a bonus to catch the Speaker's eye, that I've spoken in every debate on ———— for the last twelve years. And, because one's given one's views constantly on the subject, illogically this increases the likelihood that one will be asked to trot them out yet again.

If you specialise you accumulate a great deal more knowledge. You're asked to give your views in your own party and so on. If you become an all-rounder, there is a great danger of becoming a bore.

One Conservative, however, who had hitherto been a specialist, reported sadly that he found himself — 'unfortunately' — becoming an all-rounder.

Why unfortunately?
Because I think it's a wrong approach to the job today in the present House of Commons, when practically everybody around you is specialising.

Then why become one?

I keep trying to stop it. I can't: it's like my hair going grey. My problem is an unquenchable thirst for what goes on in the House, and the House is an all-round place. There's something different every day.

Oddly, the one Labour MP who confessed to being an all-rounder regretted, on the contrary, not being a specialist.

I don't make a virtue of not specialising. Rather the reverse. I feel in fact that one of the most valuable things a Member of Parliament can do is make the kind of detailed, nuts-and-bolts contribution that only a specialist can make. The rest of us get het up about pensions, but we're not prepared to do the spade work.

Most of the MPs regarded the trend towards specialisation as, on the whole, desirable as well as inevitable. 'We are only effective', a Labour Member maintained, 'to the extent that we get expertise in one or more subjects.' But some of the more experienced Members, especially on the Conservative side, were doubtful.

You tend inevitably to become a little academic when you specialise, and when you become a little academic (particularly if you're not one) you tend to feel yourself a newly-made intellectual. And what you're driven hard up against then is the purely instinctual. Now I give the instinctual a tremendously high place in politics. I think that when we cease to be instinctual and become too dedicated to the specialists — and think that research, and the poll, and the count must precede every decision — then we may as well pack up.

I believe that a generalist is probably a better politician than a specialist. If you become a specialist and ignore the general, you cease to be influential over the broad political spectrum: you cease to influence your party to do right or wrong. If you become a specialist, you tend to drop out.

And it was a Labour MP who pointed out that it is not the narrow specialists who get to the top.

What was Harold Wilson's specialty? What was Hugh Gaitskell's? What are Michael Foot's, Tony Crosland's? Let's look at the people who've made it to the top. 'Young man, specialise.' What did these characters specialise in? Nothing.

It may indeed be that to become too highly specialised is to commit oneself to being a career backbencher.

One Labour Member, however, made the point that it is possible for someone to be something of an expert in a particular field without confining himself to that field exclusively. He insisted that, while the *specialist*/generalist dichotomy may be a real one, the *expert*/generalist dichotomy is not.

Frank Allaun has a mighty range of interests. It just so happens that the one he's best known for is housing; and, if I had a question that I wanted to raise on housing, who would I go to, straight away, but Frank Allaun? But to suggest, if anybody is suggesting, that Frank Allaun is dealing with housing to the exclusion of everything else, we know round this table that that just isn't true.

Another Labour Member maintained that the true expert in the House of Commons is a much rarer bird that many of his colleagues were making out.

The number of parliamentary experts who can really hold their own with experts outside, in my opinion, is very, very small. You get the occasional one like ———, but the point about ——— is that he's specialised in the House in things he was already an expert on outside. That's quite untypical.

Whether or not they are true experts or even specialists in any very strict sense, most MPs do have two or three subjects that they mainly think about and speak about. Many are simply maintaining in the House interests that they had already acquired outside.

I've always been interested in economics, and I just naturally gravitated towards economic subjects when I came in.

I was a professional man outside. I solemnly resolved not to get caught up in the concerns of my profession inside: I would just get bored. But that's precisely what happened – at least for a long time. Everyone expected me to do my thing, so I just had to.

Most Members develop interests in connection with their constituencies. And often new developments in their lives outside the House have repercussions inside.

I was asked to go on a hospital board two years ago. Nothing to do with the House. You go on a hospital board, you begin to learn about the mechanics of the National Health Service and its administration and so on, and suddenly you feel prompted to take some action in Parliament about it. It's like being in business; I'm in business in the NHS.

One of the group of MPs who took a notable interest in Biafra was very candid about how he took the cause up.

I was looking for an issue. I think part of my feeling at that time was: 'Look, I've been sitting in this place for two years, and so far it's not been awfully interesting really, and I may be out of it in two years' time, so why not have a go?'

One day a certain Nigerian, an Ibo, who was a constituent of mine, came to see me. This would have been in July 1967, the war having started in June. And he drew a map of Nigeria, or rather of Africa, and he said, 'Look, this is the situation.' I'm slightly making fun of myself, because I had been following it and I had one or two Nigerian friends. But it was he, I think, more than anything else, who made me take it up. I then quickly became aware of the highly unsatisfactory attitude of the British Government.

But of course, for those in government or with front-bench responsibilities on the opposition side, concentration on a subject is often a simple consequence of their being asked to take it up.

The fact is that, when the leader of your party, whether you're in government or out of it, turns round to you and says, 'Will you be Parliamentary Secretary to the Ministry of Works?' or, as Harold did to me, 'Will you do Posts and Telecommunications?' – about which I'm bound to say my ignorance was immense and my interest minimal – what do you do? You say yes. So then for eighteen months or two years you become interested in stamps and broadcasting.
Very good you were at it too.

Specialties are like Topsy, they grow upon one. I'm now an expert on agriculture. This would have been thought a great joke a few years ago. I came to the House determined to achieve something in foreign affairs and something in education, since which time I've been subsidising pigs. It grows on one.

I happen to be interested in overseas aid. I was asked to become a PPS [parliamentary private secretary] at a certain stage in my political career and therefore I had to become more interested in overseas aid.

The degree of specialisation to be found in the modern House of Commons – and the extent of it can be exaggerated even now – means that many backbench MPs are reading and thinking about their subjects more or less all the time. They read the newspapers with an eye to news items bearing on their interests; they visit the appropriate foreign countries; they attend, especially if they are Conservatives, the appropriate party committees. Even non-specialists inhabit a world of almost continuous political talk and reading. Preparation for taking part in discussion and debate is therefore almost never a matter of starting from scratch: in some way or other most MPs are preparing themselves most of the time.

I would have thought that the accumulation of the information that you may eventually use is not necessarily a deliberate act, but something that is continuous. One might want a little more detail when one knows the subject of a specific debate – just a few facts to illustrate a point – but one is always gathering things in.

At one of the Labour dinners, one of the party's spokesmen was asked roughly how long he would spend preparing a front-bench speech that he was satisfied with – one of about half an hour. The frontbencher found the question impossible to answer:

This is my whole way of life. If I answered you, I could say either twenty-four hours a day or five minutes, because you're absorbing material at every moment.

MPs do have to do some preparation for specific meetings and debates all the same, even if it is only a matter of 'a few facts to illustrate a point.' One Labour Member was quite clear where he could not turn for help.

We don't, most of us, have research assistants. We get little support from the Labour Party – although that's not their fault; they don't have the money.

For him and for many others on both sides, preparation is largely a do-it-yourself affair.

Library probably, press cutting service, research assistant there. I get my secretary, when she has time, to do a certain amount of devilling. All this assuming I don't have what I want on file myself, and I keep, as far as I can on our limited resources, a reasonable subject file. Anything that comes up in my reading that I think may be of future interest I cut out or photocopy and put by.

Many Members, again on both sides, laid stress on the importance of experience in a field, and of having a network of personal contacts.

Most of it is experience. I've written, alone or with other people, every party pamphlet on ———— for the last ten years. By now I'm beginning to take some of the points on board.

One relies a lot on contacts one has. If you cite, say, Northern Ireland, then I think that is the kind of issue where there are various individuals — whether they've been serving over there, or whether they're journalists who've been covering it — who've got a lot of very detailed information. And one would get on the telephone.

I have a circle of friends and acquaintances — I suppose it's fairly wide by now — and I automatically know, when a subject's coming up, who to ask round for a drink. He's the man who will tell me — providing I don't ever say that I've seen him — what is going to make my speech effective.

A Conservative reckoned to read and telephone, but also to go round and see people.

Once I wanted to introduce a debate on overseas aid — an all-day debate when I'd come top in the ballot. I got in touch with various people on the phone and went to see some of them. One of them is now the President of the CBI. I wanted to know what private industry thought so I went to see him. And one doesn't have difficulty getting access to such people if you know them at all. And in a few minutes, ten minutes, you get very good value.

These personal contacts frequently take the form of continuing relationships, with organisations as well as individuals. In fact all but one or two of the MPs at the dinners reported that they had some kind of continuing association with at least one outside body, often with several.

There are two organisations with which I have very close contact: the National Society for the Prevention of Cruelty to Children and the National Association of Parish Councils. They approached me and I agreed to give them what assistance I could, on the strict understanding that my responsibility mainly would be in the parliamentary field.

There is one embassy with which I have a close connection and that is the ————Embassy — a special case where, arising from a complete accident of chance, which years ago gave me an interest in that country and a certain sympathy with their point of view, I have felt that there is a need on our side of the House to improve contacts with them.

I have kept entirely in touch with all the disabled organisations. They know what they're talking about because the people who run them are disabled.

I'm a lawyer and I practise, and therefore to a certain extent the groups I keep in touch with are things like the Criminal Bar Association, the Bar Council and so on.

If you're interested in defence, you make it your business to have contacts with the people at the Institute for Strategic Studies.

Although the overlap between the two parties in most fields is considerable — they have common contacts with a wide range of charities, professions, embassies and research bodies like the ISS — Conservative MPs obviously have especially close links with business, Labour with the trade unions. It does not take much imagination to guess which of the following quotations are from Tories, which from Labour Members.

I go about once a year to a dinner given by the shipping and shipbuilding group of MPs, where we invite the Chamber of Shipping along and the shipbuilders, and we dine, rather like this, and discuss the whole range of shipping matters.

For some odd reason I'm invited from time to time to have dinner with the Timber Association. A Member of Parliament gives a dinner, invites the timber top ten along and invites ten MPs to discuss the problems of timber. It's fascinating to hear about timber in building and so on — the developments.

My union and I have been in close, continuous contact all through the present steel situation. I also see a lot of the other unions and local trades councils.

The people I keep in the closest touch with are the shop stewards in the two biggest factories in my area. For example, during the entire difficult period 1968-70 I used to have a meeting every six weeks with the shop stewards from ————. About thirty used to come up on a Saturday morning every month or so, and we would discuss politics.

The drug industry has been frightened to death of being nationalised for ten years, and I've got by heart now the speech they make to Members of Parliament about their function and why they shouldn't be nationalised.

The extent to which business contacts are only with Tory

MPs, however, should not be overstated. A minority of Labour Members are in business themselves; more important,
some contacts are with industries as a whole and not just with
the management or trade union side alone.

It is fairly clear what these outside groups hope to gain from
MPs: the asking of parliamentary questions, the moving of
amendments, a quiet word in the ear of the minister. But MPs
are equally clear about what they gain from the groups, at least
where the groups are reasonably well run and efficient.

I have a brief from the Consumers' Association in my pocket at the
moment for the debate tomorrow. It does contain a couple of points
which I would not in fact have come across if they hadn't been drawn
to my attention.

The clergyman who is secretary, I think, of the Church of England's
Council on Betting and Gaming knows more about football pools
and all forms of betting and gaming than any other person I've ever
met. He worked in co-operation with both sides on the Betting and
Gaming Bill, and his information was sharp and objective. He's a
man of the utmost rectitude, but he could tell people how roulette
ought to be run, he knew all the Continental systems — he had a vast
influence on the outcome.

Outside groups provide information. They can also provide
detailed briefings on amendments when bills are in committee,
and sometimes even the amendments themselves.

On the Industry Bill I had a lot to do with the CBI. I didn't agree
with them all the way, but their amendments were very well argued.
Of course they go so far as actually to draft amendments for you to
consider putting forward — which is a constructive help and certainly
not despised by any opposition, because they're well thought out.

In 1968, on the committee stage of the Race Relations Bill, there was
a body set up called Equal Rights, which did a very good briefing job
of Members on the committee, and they were extremely well organised. Their views about the shape the legislation should take happened to accord with mine to a very large extent, and every morning
at 9.30 when the committee was about to sit one was briefed on what
was coming up that day: both orally and with pieces of paper and so
on. If they happened to be pushing a particular point that I disagreed
with, I opted out. When I agreed with them, I did what I could. It
was a total service: I went into that committee briefed on every
amendment that was going to come up in a way that I've only ever

seen a minister briefed or an opposition spokesman.

But not all interest groups are as well organised as this one. Especially at the Conservative dinners, some tart remarks were made about the incompetence of many of the groups, including some of the better known ones.

The RSPCA campaign which is going on at the moment about the export of live animals to Europe infuriates me, because they've only just now launched it even though there is nothing now — since we're in the EEC — the Government can actually do. The whole campaign is absolutely pointless. It irritates Members and produces bad feeling between Members of Parliament and constituents who have got caught up in the campaign.

Can I add to that? I once got a letter, not from the RSPCA but from somebody who obviously had something to do with it, saying they would not vote for me unless I supported a particular motion. They were obviously quite unaware that I was not only a sponsor of the motion but had actually written it myself.

On one classic occasion I got a letter that actually had 'Draft Letter No. 4' typed at the top. Somebody had just topped and tailed it and sent it to me.

The inept ones don't only make one laugh: they make one very irritated — for example, with a brief that arrives just before the debate takes place or even, as not uncommonly happens, after it's over.

There is a good deal of controversy, and always will be, about what sorts of outside contacts are strictly ethical. On the one hand, outside groups provide valuable services to Members and make them more effective critics of government. On the other, MPs could misuse their parliamentary position for the groups' benefit, and also for their own. Some Labour Members were of the view that the payment of fees for representing groups in Parliament should never be allowed, even when the association between Member and group is well known. No Member of Parliament, however, can sever all his links with 'the interests' — as one Conservative explained.

We're all human beings, not just politicians. Some of the most important influences on us come from our family background, our church, if we belong to one, the way we earn our living. We happen to have adopted a child in our family, and so questions about adoption and adoption societies will from now on, you know, have a particular entrée for me. This sort of thing is often underrated: these sorts of accidental influences. Also, we are in contact with vast numbers of organisations simply because they send us pieces of paper. And then I'm sure all of us around here are involved in voluntary bodies and this sort of thing. I happen to be chairman of a housing association, so naturally during the committee on the Housing Finance Bill not only my own association but all the others tended to centre in on me with their advice. These things are changing and shifting all the time, but they're always there.

Although it is up to the individual MP to decide what sort of Member he will be, his success in making an impact will depend on his ability to exert influence. Chapters 4 and 5 were concerned with the possibilities of exerting influence through one's party. The next two chapters deal with what the Member can accomplish in the House of Commons itself.

7 The Floor of the House

Most people, when they think of the House of Commons, still think of the high ceilinged chamber and the rows of green benches. Most MPs still seem to think of them too, even though the debates that take place on the floor of the House are no longer as important as they once were (or are said to have been) and even though much of the work of the House is now done in committees upstairs. The main purpose of this part of our discussion, indeed, was to find out how far MPs believe that what goes on in the chamber is still important.

The two main things that go on in the chamber are debates, either on proposed pieces of legislation or on motions of one kind or another, and the asking and answering of parliamentary questions. Most of the discussion was focussed on the set-piece debate, but several Members were anxious that the usefulness of the parliamentary question should not be forgotten.

Many Members trade on the question and regard it as infinitely more effective, provided it is skilfully constructed, than the speech. You can achieve seven-tenths of all we're talking about if you think ahead and make sure you're near the top of the list for questions. And then, having thought out the question, you think out a supplementary.

Question time is particularly important and influential. I'm not sure it should be, but I'm quite sure it is. You get much more publicity per line for a question than you will ever get per line for a speech. You get an opportunity to influence the whole House when it's at its fullest. A new Member can find out who people are more quickly by going to question time than by doing anything else.

And one Labour Member – generally credited with being a phenomenally successful constituency Member – recounted how he had won a major (to him) battle with the parliamentary question as almost his only weapon.

The Minister was going to let an airplane factory in my constituency close. The factory employed nearly four hundred people, so I put down two hundred detailed questions in the House – two hundred! I

brought the ministry to a complete stop. So ——— fetched me up in
the middle of the night and says, 'What the bloody hell do you think
you're doing.' I knew I was winning because he lost his temper. He
said to me, 'I'm going to see Harold [then still Prime Minister] about
you in the morning.' And I said, 'Well, Fred, I just hope you get
there before I get to the Table Office to put down some more questions.' And he didn't — because I sat up all night and in the morning
put down another fifty. In the end, Fred fetches me in again and says,
'All right, you win, I give up.' Four hundred jobs, and I saved them.

   Parliamentary questions, under the rules of the House, must
be addressed to particular ministers. Interventions in debate
must likewise be addressed formally to the Speaker or chairman. But in neither case — certainly very seldom in the case of
contributions to debate — does the person being formally addressed necessarily constitute the audience the Member is
really trying to reach. On most occasions, Members speaking
in the House will be trying to reach someone — but whom? To
find out who Members see as constituting their audience is to
discover something about how they believe they exercise influence (if they believe they do exercise it). Once again, the
differences within the parties were much more striking than
the differences between them.

   There is an awareness, of course, that one is trying to reach
different people on different occasions. As a Labour Member
put it:

There's no general answer to this. It depends on the bill, the subject
you're speaking on. The tenor of my remarks depends entirely on the
measure. For example, if I were talking on the Children's and Young
Persons' Bill, I would probably be talking to Mark Carlisle [Minister
of State at the Home Office] because he's a reasonable minister. If,
on the other hand, I were talking on the Housing Finance Bill, I
wouldn't really be expecting to get any change out of the Government, so I would be talking to people outside.
Who outside?
Well, certainly always to my own constituents. I never forget that.
Most of us are hopeful that the BBC will pick it up and that some of
the national papers will. There's probably not an MP who's spoken
during the day who doesn't go home in the car at night, if it's a
reasonably early finish, and switch the radio on to see if they've got a
mention in *Today in Parliament.*

But although most Members were aware of having different audiences in mind on different occasions, most of them seemed to have an, as it were, preferred audience: someone or some group whom they were much more likely to be addressing than another. In several cases — but fewer than one might have supposed — the preferred audience was the Government.

Subjectively, I tend to feel as if I'm talking to the Government.

On the bill we were talking about a moment ago, I was addressing the Government. I was saying to the Government: 'Look, by your own standards you're talking nonsense. You've got certain objectives: clearly you're not going to achieve them: you cannot show me by any argument you can produce that you are going to achieve them by these methods.' I was talking to the Government and, indeed, I don't really know who else one's talking to most of the time.

First there's the minister. Somebody mentioned Mark Carlisle so let's personalise the minister into Mark Carlisle. He's a Minister whom on some subjects — if you talk persuasively enough — you feel you can get to: to change his mind. He'll go back to his office and say, 'Look, there does seem to be a point here. Look at it and bring me back something.' Whether talking in the House or writing to the person, it's the same device.

Several of those who did not see themselves as addressing the Government directly were trying to reach the Government nevertheless, but via the civil service. It is probably significant that it was the ex-ministers who tended to think in these terms.

It's no good talking to the minister on the front bench. He ignores it, even if he understands it. What one is trying to do is put the fear of God into the civil servants.

One despairs of influencing ministers, most of whom seem to have briefs and who are doggedly going to get whatever they want. When I speak, I speak to the civil servants who have so much of the power.

The senior civil servants, they're the chaps I'm after. The thing is getting senior civil servants to come to the minister three days after the debate saying, 'Minister, we ought to point out to you: Mr ———— had a point in that speech he made. The permanent secretary was meaning to have a word with you before the debate, but unfortunately ... The bill is defective and we shall have to make an amendment in committee.' Now you've achieved something.

No one at the dinners saw the Members on the other side of the House as their primary audience; indeed most of them did not mention the other side at all. But a few were at least concerned not to ignore them. One Member could not quite put his finger on why not.

I'm not sure why it is, but when I'm speaking in the House I always hope that something I say will strike a chord with the people opposite. I don't expect them to agree with me, but I like to have some feeling of rapport with them.

Probably this feeling is more common than Members like to admit; after all, one has to be unusually hard-hearted to enjoy confronting an audience that is wholly indifferent or hostile. There is the point, too, that from time to time one may need the help of one's political opponents.

You may have a different target if you write off the minister. I've got something at the moment that I want to achieve – it's my only objective this winter – and I can't achieve it directly with the minister: I can only do it by winning over a few of the opposition people on the committee. And I think I will.

I took part in a debate last year on a clause in the Finance Bill. We organised twenty-five speakers from both sides of the House. Because so many speakers from both parties were united against the clause, the Chancellor had to give way.

Several Members were very slightly mystified by the original question and found themselves thinking aloud about the answer. One concluded that he typically talked to a number of different audiences and a number of different people.

I would have thought my speeches have mainly been addressed to the 'establishment', though I'm not quite sure whether these are civil servants or ministers. If they're ministers, it's certainly not for an acceptance and a reply right there: it's for something in the future. I'm not sure, but the people who talked about the civil servants are probably quite right.

Then I think there's also a degree to which your audience is the local press and the people in your constituency. I hope I'm always creating an image of the sort of person I am and the sort of views that I have. But certainly that – the constituency – is a very secondary consideration as far as I'm concerned.

Almost everyone agreed that he had his constituency in mind

from time to time, but it was clear that none saw his constituency as his primary audience and several Members emphasised how speeches blatantly intended for constituency consumption ('for the folks back home') could be disastrous in the House.

One possible audience for speeches in Parliament is the outside groups mentioned in the last chapter. Certainly most groups pay close attention to debates in Parliament affecting their industry or profession. One might suppose that MPs generally would be consciously concerned to convey their views to these groups. In fact it seems that some are, some are not.

Why should we wish to do this? You are there when the decisions are taken. I grant you it's gratifying if the professions with which we're mixed up perceive that we're *simpatico* — and, not only that, but very comprehending of the practical details that involve them — but it doesn't get you very far, except that they regard you as a friend in the camp.

No, I don't agree. I find myself often doing this. Only the other day I was visited by some steel workers from Wales, and I said, 'Why do you come all this way to see me?' 'Oh', they said, six of them, 'because we see from Hansard that you speak on steel.' And I had been speaking on steel, and they'd spotted it, or been advised by their union, and come to see me about it. I'm very conscious of this sort of running dialogue with people outside.

Almost all back-bench MPs must wonder from time to time whether they are actually reaching anybody, or whether it is even worth trying. A Labour Member reckoned that most of the time the only people listening to him were 'the two men up behind the clock': the Hansard reporters. But it was a Conservative who came closest to saying that the whole thing is a waste of time.

I'm not interested in what the House thinks about my speeches. I couldn't give two pins for what my colleagues think about them: I say what I want to say. If somebody says afterwards, 'What a good speech you made', I'm delighted; but, if nobody said anything, although I'd be disappointed, it wouldn't bother me. A writer doesn't write his books for his readers: he writes them for himself. If you happen to like his book, splendid; if not, then that's just too bad. And anyway the great question in one's mind is: who is one supposed to be influencing anyway?

A Labour MP put the same point even more eloquently, though in general he was a more sanguine person than his Conservative colleague.

I'm grinning because, as you've all been talking, I've been thinking of the last scene of *Marino Faliero*, a much underestimated closet drama by Lord Byron. In the last scene, which takes place inside the Doge's Palace, they lock the population outside. Poor old Marino Faliero ascends the scaffold, but the crowd whom he's tried to lead to liberty and all the rest of it are locked out. He starts to speak, and they say, 'But no one can hear you.' And he says, 'I speak to time and to eternity.' I sometimes feel in the House of Commons that we are speaking only to time and to eternity.

To some extent, the differences that were evident on this subject merely reflect MPs' varying preoccupations and their consciousness that, as was said earlier, one has different audiences in mind on different occasions. Nevertheless, the fact that there was so much disagreement, and that some Members did not seem too clear who normally they were talking to, may suggest that Members of Parliament are no longer (if they ever were) entirely certain what the role of the House of Commons is, or what part they themselves play in it. The thought would almost certainly have occurred to anyone listening to the discussion that at least some speeches in the House of Commons are made simply because the House of Commons is a place for making speeches in. And even those Members who make speeches genuinely in order to be heard are not always sure whether anyone is listening. Be that as it may, a similar element of disagreement and uncertainty was again evident when the discussion turned away from the question of whom MPs are talking to and towards the question of exactly whom or what their talk influences.

Parliamentary debates serve a number of functions which are separate to an extent from the declared purposes of the Members who take part in them. One of the chief of these is to establish, or at least to influence, MPs' reputations with their colleagues. No speech in the House of Commons is ever made for the express purpose either of making the reputation of the speaker or of unmaking the reputation of an opponent. Yet the totality of a man's speeches — and his questions, interventions, replies and so on — is bound to play a part in determining

what his colleagues think of him. On this point there was no
disagreement.

Especially vulnerable are the reputations of ministers. One
Conservative remarked:

This is terribly important – even more so today because of the way
ministers are organised in these big conglomerate departments, which
make it much more difficult for them to shine on their own. I always
remember when Peter Walker first came before the House at question time with his team, and one watched to see what would happen.
I think of about twenty-five questions that were answered Peter
Walker answered only about three; the others were delegated down
the line to his Ministers of State. Yet there was no question in my
mind but that Peter Walker was in charge of those ministers, and
very much in charge of the ministry. There you saw a politician – very practised, very much a political person, but wholly in-
experienced in Cabinet – completely in command of the scene in the
House of Commons.

Another said:

We had a superb example this afternoon in Keith Joseph. He had
some very difficult ones, both from the Opposition and from our own
back benches, but he was as tough as hell in the politest possible way
and never once did he offend anybody. He is the supreme example of
how a minister can become an influence in the House.

The Conservatives, it must be said, were not quite so flattering
about everybody on their front bench.

Influence on the reputations of individuals is one thing; influence on actual Government policies and decisions is another. If there was something approaching consensus at the
dinners on the one, on the other there was a good deal of
disagreement. Members on both sides could cite instances
where backbenchers had indeed had influence, but without any
recourse whatever to the floor of the House. A senior Conservative told this story:

I happened to be standing next to the ticker-tape machine in the
Lobby of the House years ago, when a report came in that the Government had decided to make available to the Indian Air Force,
through the United Nations, some thousand-pound bombs for use in
Katanga. As I watched this come up on the tape, I happened to be
standing next to a minister, who was more or less responsible for
this. I said, 'What on earth do you think you're doing?' He turned to

me and said, 'Oh, I don't think our people will be much concerned
about this, do you?' I said, 'I most certainly do.' And on the spot we
had an argument in which I got angrier and angrier and angrier.

That was on Friday. On Saturdy I spent quite a portion of the
day ringing up every Sunday political correspondent I knew, saying
there would be fury about this, simply on the basis that I reckoned
there would be a fair number of people who would share my views.
And in fact a considerable proportion of the Sunday press did lead
their front pages on restiveness in the Conservative Party on this
particular point.

On the Monday, when we came back, there was indeed fury. Now,
whether there would have been fury if there hadn't been the stories in
the Sunday papers – if I hadn't spent most of Saturday informing
their political correspondents – I don't know. But I was interested to
see that Harold Macmillan devotes several pages of his memoirs to
the difficult situation which suddenly arose. Well, except to the Minister, I said not a single word on this – on the floor of the House or
anywhere else.

A Labour Member told a different story, but with the same
point.

When we were in government, I played a part, and I think an effective part, in keeping open a shipyard on the north side of Teesmouth.
I was enabled to play that part because I happened to be appointed to
the working party that Tony Wedgwood Benn set up to study the
future of a particular shipyard that was due for closure. We didn't
make a great deal of progress on the working party, from its point of
view; but I got hold of a tremendous number of facts because of the
cross-examination to which we could subject various bigwigs in the
shipbuilding industry and so on.

As a result, at a later time, when the Northern Group of Labour
Members met Tony Wedgwood Benn, I was able to lead off with a
brief I'd prepared entirely by myself, establishing a good technical
case, a good economic case, a good hard cash case for keeping that
yard open. Tony was constantly referring to his senior civil servants,
so in a sense I was talking directly to them, and they were having to
confirm what I said. And Wedgwood Benn came down in fact in our
favour. Now, that's one of the few real successes that I've been able
to claim personally, and the thing was that it was done entirely outside the chamber. I didn't speak a word in the chamber, but it was
one of the best things I've done.

To show that things can be accomplished entirely outside
the chamber, however, is not to show that things cannot also

be accomplished inside it. Whether or not they can – and, if they can, whether the things that can be accomplished in the chamber are worth accomplishing – was the subject of a long and sometimes rather heated discussion at one of the Labour dinners. It was opened by a Member who would not normally be thought of as an extremist.

I do not believe in the chamber of the House of Commons. I believe that most of what happens there is a farce, and that the whole thing is one remove – several removes – from reality. It's acted out, it's stylised, it's for the benefit of the people in the press gallery, and the real decisions are taken elsewhere. As long as one relies on the chamber, one doesn't have a House of Commons: one has a House of Rubber Stamps.

That's, if I may say so, an absolutely ludicrous position. I would not trade the chamber of the House of Commons – the floor of the House of Commons – for anything, because the essence of the British system is a confrontation between the party that is in government and the party that is out of government.

For what? For what ends?

I think we're getting confused. I've never heard a minister or ex-minister say, quite solemnly, that a parliamentary question or an adjournment debate or something like that, affecting a constituent or the affairs of a company or the activities of this and that, is quite meaningless. On this sort of thing, the floor of the House is very important – no question about that. If, as I have, you've seen the green ministerial folders coming down, flagged 'urgent', and going through all the processes, you know that on this type of thing the Member of Parliament is quite a strong character provided he's persistent.

Now on the big questions of politics – on the 'macro-politics' if you want to call it that – take, for example, the House of Lords business three years ago: the behaviour of the Labour Party and the right wing of the Tories. The fact is that our Chief Whip had to go and say to the Cabinet, 'I cannot deliver a sufficient majority to carry a guillotine motion on the House of Lords Bill.' In other words, the Government had lost control of the House of Commons on a major measure and had to drop it.

Or – I'm not going into the merits of it – take the bill that never happened, the one on industrial relations, after *In Place of Strife*. Remember that that bill, or that non-bill, followed the last Prices and Incomes Bill, and the rebellion on that had demoralised the Government; so, when they got another rebellion, they retreated. And that

was an important thing; no one imagines it wasn't. Likewise, after the
trouble Heath had with his own party abolishing RPM [resale price
maintenance] in 1964, the Tory Government decided not to bring in
a lot of contentious bills that they'd had in mind for that session. It's
not only the bills of the moment: it's the bills that come after that are
affected. I just don't agree about the House of Commons being pow-
erless, irrelevant or having no place at all.

Do I agree or disagree? I think mainly disagree. I think the House of
Commons doesn't count much in the decision-making process with
the rare exceptions of things like the ones that have just been mentioned. Those are very rare indeed – they're the exceptions that
prove the rule – and it's only when people get really het up about a
subject that anything happens.

Contrary to what one might have supposed, it was not only
Labour Members who were as disenchanted as the first and
last speakers above. An almost exactly similar discussion took
place at a Conservative dinner, with much the same points of
view being expressed just as vehemently. One Tory insisted
again and again: 'I personally cannot escape a sense of futility.'
Both discussions were inconclusive, but what did seem to
emerge – apart from the fact that a number of Members on
both sides are extremely discontented with Parliament – was
that, on rare occasions when a sufficiently large number of
Government backbenchers are sufficiently steamed up, the
House of Commons can prevent a Government from doing
something, or can make it think twice about even attempting
to do something. What the House cannot easily do is act crea-
tively, either in the sense of forcing a Government to adopt
one policy rather than another or in the sense of causing it to
adopt an entirely new policy. Events may do these things; the
House of Commons, as organised at present, cannot.

To concentrate on particular decisions and particular incidents, however, may be to miss part of the point. A former
Labour minister argued forcefully that a Government's mo-
rale, and its ability to get its way with its own backbenchers,
could suffer if over a period of time it was consistently shown
to be unable to hold its own in debate.

It's desperately important always to present the best possible argument in favour of whatever it is you're arguing for. The argument as
such is an important thing. Although the House of Commons is not

capable of initiating power, it is capable of withdrawing power; it is capable of eroding the position of a Government; it is capable of producing, indeed, a position in which, because it is no longer winning the arguments on the floor of the House, it loses the confidence of its own backbenchers and cannot do certain things it wants to – like pass the Industrial Relations Bill that was referred to.

Because such situations are easier to feel than to describe, their importance may be overlooked.

Time as a factor was also mentioned in a slightly different connection by two Tory MPs. They were refuting the view that, because few individual speeches in the House make a measurable impact on policy, therefore no speeches in the House matter.

I suspect there is a time lag in this. It follows from what someone was saying about talking to the civil service. The thing about civil servants is that there can be a follow-on at a later stage. You don't expect anything to happen straight away. All of these things – speaking, threatening the withdrawal of one's vote, and so on – have the effect, not necessarily of changing a decision, but of moving it a bit.

Another Conservative, a more experienced one, was more emphatic.

I would like to come back to this point about the Member of Parliament's not influencing the Government. If we look at it completely statically, then we're right: they have the whips and we don't have much influence. But allow for a little passage of time, and things change. It is not forgotten what certain Members of Parliament have been thinking over a period. Only a year ago I made three speeches in a row on the future of the coal industry. In the third speech I said to my own front bench: what is the good of a Member of Parliament speaking from this side of the House to his own front bench if they will never listen? And now it seems that they were listening all along: the policy's changed. And within a period of twelve months there's been a change of view. I'm not saying it's due to a single individual's speeches; the situation has changed. But I find it hard to believe it made no difference to have people on our side taking a particular line.

However important the floor of the House may be – and some Members, as we have seen, do not think it is important at all – there was general agreement that, if the chamber was ever the sole focus of parliamentary life, it no longer is. On the day of one of the Labour dinners, the Parliamentary Labour Party voted not to send representatives to join the British delegation at the European Parliament in Strasbourg. One of the MPs who went to the party meeting observed:

It seems to me that the most important vote we've had since October didn't take place in the chamber of the House of Commons at all. It took place in Room 14 this morning. It was of tremendous importance to the political structure, not only of the Labour Party, but within Britain as a whole.

A number of Conservatives also saw the various party groupings as effective rivals to the chamber, and one senior Member, asked how far the proceedings in the chamber influence events, replied: 'It must be right to say less than they did.'

We still live in two worlds really, without having chosen between them. One is the world of the select committees and so on, and most of us reckon to do a lot of work through that. And the other is the chamber, and one thinks of what one can do there. We all know where the weight has shifted, and you can't do everything at once so you shift too. It follows that the audience in the chamber, which can make an effective speech sound more effective, is no longer there. I think that certain figures — Enoch Powell obviously, and there are one or two others on the other side — can still make a speech which is picked up and which makes its mark; and people say, 'That was a remarkable contribution to the debate.' But it doesn't happen very often. I'm rather pessimistic.

All this said, it remains true that it is virtually impossible, in fact, to isolate the influence of the chamber and to separate it out from the influence of the various party meetings and of the 'world of select committees' referred to by the Conservative just quoted. Another Conservative reverted several times to the point that the activities of the House of Commons are, and ought to be seen as being, an interlocking whole.

I regard the parliamentary speech as only one element in a whole number of factors which you bring into account in your campaign, whatever it might be. There's the parliamentary speech, there's the parliamentary question, there's the motion on the order paper, there's the committee upstairs, and there's the use of the press and public opinion outside. You've got to use them all together to bring your influence to bear to achieve the end you seek.

The next chapter deals with another of this Member's 'whole number of factors': with the House of Commons committee system.

8 Upstairs

The committee system of the House of Commons resembles nothing so much as a peculiarly elaborate Heath Robinson contraption, with at any given moment something like thirty-five committees and sub-committees performing almost as many different functions. Understanding how it works is not made any easier by the fact that its most important parts have names − 'standing' and 'select' committees − which give no indication of what they are or how they fit into the whole. Partly for these reasons, the work of House committees is probably the aspect of the House of Commons least understood by those outside.

The fact is, however, that the work of the House could not be done without committees; that all MPs take their importance for granted (even if some do not want their functions extended); and that the committee system is, in its essentials, a good deal less complicated than a formal organisation chart would suggest. The discussion at the dinners was concerned partly with how far back-bench Members can influence Governments working through the committee system as it exists at present, and partly with whether the present system ought to be replaced by a new one. The extent of dissatisfaction expressed with the present system was considerable.

The phrase 'standing committee' is misleading. Standing committees in the House of Commons are permanently in being in the sense that they are never formally dissolved; but their membership changes constantly. Their purpose is to examine legislation, and as each new bill comes forward the entire membership of the committee to which it is sent is renewed − rather in the way that the same form in a school consists each year of new pupils. The membership of the standing committee on a particular bill will certainly include some Members who specialise in the bill's subject matter; but it is unlikely to consist solely of specialists. Standing committees examine in detail bills that have already been read a second time − that is, approved in principle − by the whole

House. They function very much, in fact, as miniature Houses of Commons. Ministers and Opposition spokesmen confront each other across the committee room, and bills are debated clause by clause just as they would have been in the full House. Standing committees do not call witnesses or cross-examine ministers and civil servants. And votes are not free votes; the whips are on.

It quickly emerged at our dinners that, as so often, what goes on in the formal proceedings of a standing committee need not be by any means all that is going on at the committee stage. MPs on both sides told stories of back-bench activity that took place out of the hearing of the Hansard reporters. A Labour Member described how he had conducted his opposition to some clauses of a bill brought in by the Labour Government.

The bill was controversial, but not in party terms, and several Opposition amendments came up which I had a lot of sympathy with. I rarely made a speech, but I happened to be sitting immediately behind the Minister's PPS and occasionally I would lean forward and say, 'Look, I don't think I'm going to be able to support you on this.' And he would pass a note to the Minister, and we'd get a bit of a concession: he said he'd look at it again, or he might even accept the Opposition amendment. The point is that sometimes you can achieve more by not speaking than by speaking.

According to two Conservatives, ministers often recognise the need to make concessions in committee if a bill has been attacked on second reading by backbenchers on the Government side.

If it's been a bad second reading, the minister will see the writing on the wall. Very often, between the second reading and the committee, he will invite the Members on his own side who will be on the committee to come round for a general talk. They will stress to him where in fact they will have trouble coming along with him, and he will say, 'Well, we'll certainly bear that in mind.' And then you're apt to find that certain Government amendments are tabled. That sort of preliminary talk can make all the difference to the shape of a bill.

Recently, when the 1972 Industry Bill went to the House, there was very little support on the Government benches for it, very little. I was one, I think, of only two Members who spoke in support, and there was a lot of criticism – hardly surprisingly since it was a case of the Government's going through a 180-degree turn. Then the Bill as drafted encountered a lot of opposition from our benches when it came up to the standing committee, which I was on. But probably this opposition by itself wouldn't have caused the Government to alter the Bill; the real opposition came from the President of the CBI, who made a speech one weekend. That speech caused a certain coalescence, if I may put it like that, on the Conservative back benches, and the Government then put down a number of amendments, which were accepted.

Most changes in Government legislation are made in standing committee and, as these examples show, Government backbenchers can get changes made. This is especially true if they threaten to vote the other way: Members on both sides could cite a number of instances of successful coalitions between Government dissidents and members of the Opposition. Such coalitions, although they may be formed behind the scenes, will usually make their impact felt in public, in the committee itself, though the Government often uses its majority on the floor of the House to have committee amendments reversed. One story told by a Labour Member reflected so badly on the good faith of a well-known Conservative that the details have had to be changed completely.

I recall one case quite recently having to do with regional policy: with aid to the development areas. We've had a lot of bills on this, and one of them was in standing committee. Two industries were concerned: shipbuilding and, in my own case, coal. It so happened that the Conservative Member for a constituency near mine was prepared to come along with us on coal provided we supported him on shipbuilding. He also persuaded one of his colleagues, Sir ———— , to come along with him. It was clear the Government was going to be defeated; but, when it came to the crunch, the Government conceded on the first of the two, but it survived on the other because Sir ———— , having got what he wanted, ratted on the bargain.

On a less controversial measure, a Conservative Member simply found that he and the other side were in agreement.

It was a short committee because the Opposition didn't oppose the bill. I put forward a fair string of amendments. Some were accepted by the Government. On some the Opposition voted with me and upset the Government's majority, and the Government accepted them and put them in.

A Government may give way because, as in these instances, some of its own backbenchers are prepared to vote against it and the Government either cannot prevent them or does not feel it worth while to try to. The most famous such back-bench revolt since 1970 took place on the standing committee of the Government's Immigration Bill.

If you are clever enough to think of an amendment which for different reasons will commend itself to the Opposition and to two or three on your own side, the Government are almost bound to give way. For example, the removal of grandfathers [*laughter*] from the patrial section of the Immigration Bill found Sir George Sinclair, Enoch Powell and the Labour Party all voting on the same side — which is nice work if you can do it.

But much more often a Government gives way, not because it has to or feels it politically expedient to, but simply because it accepts that either the Opposition or the critics on its own side have got the better of the argument. Again, our MPs could give many examples, some of them on quite important pieces of legislation.

The 1965 Race Relations Bill was misconceived really from the start, wasn't it? And I think there was no argument among Members of Parliament — the people who were really interested — on both sides that it was misconceived. The then Home Secretary took it away and the officials clearly got instructions to start again.

A Conservative Member described the role he played in the committee on the Labour Government's 1968 Trade Descriptions Bill.

Our whips, I think, found that I knew something about the business of the consumer, and in particular about the promotional advertising and marketing business; and so I was asked to speak for my party on that section of the Bill. And, because I had specialist knowledge, I began to get more specialist knowledge: I began to get detailed briefing from interested bodies.
Did you in fact achieve anything?
I think I must have, because the Minister accepted certain things — amendments that I was asked to propose and did propose — not perhaps because I presented my arguments so very well, but perhaps because the base of the argument was good. I was well briefed. The Government of the time said, in effect, 'This is the situation in this particular industry, and we're prepared to accept it.'

And they did.
Was the Government ever in any serious danger of being outvoted?
No, it wasn't so much a case of that: they could have put the whips
on and carried the day. I think it was that the civil servants preparing
the Bill had not spotted these intricacies, which were much better
known to people outside Whitehall, and they recognised them at once
when somebody on the committee brought them to their attention.

However important work on standing committees is, much
of it is dry and detailed and inevitably rather tedious. One
Conservative Member had asked to be put on the Local Authority Social Services Bill.

I must say I wished I hadn't.
Why not?
I found it intolerably boring.

It can also be time-consuming – the committee stage of the
1972 Housing Finance Bill went on for a record 257
hours – and as a result not all Members are anxious to serve.

The thing that interests MPs, especially when their party is in government, is not how you get on these committees but how you keep
off. We know perfectly well there are some Members who do their
whack and some who do not. And the trouble is that those who do
not would not turn up even if they were appointed, and therefore
they aren't appointed.

A well-known dodge is to criticise the bill on second reading if
you're on the government side, or support it if you're on the opposition side. Then you can be pretty sure not to get selected!

Some bills are exceptions – the annual Finance Bill for example – but in most cases there are more places on standing
committees than there are Members keen to fill them.
It follows that, other things being equal, a Member who
does want to serve on a particular committee stands a good
chance of being 'summoned', especially if he has spoken in the
second reading debate. The Committee of Selection officially
decides who will serve, but the whips normally in practice
decide who will represent their side of the House; so an individual will usually put his name forward through them.

I wanted to get onto the Abortion Bill, and this was a difficult exercise because I was anti the Bill and, on a Friday second reading

vote, the result was in the order of 220 to 20. This set the Committee of Selection rather a problem, because so few had voted against; and it was quite a struggle. What I did was to persist with the whips, who had some responsibility even though it was a private member's bill, and to murmur to the Chairman of Selection that I actually wanted to go on. That's an unusual thing for anyone to do, so that he was sufficiently interested to listen to me. And of course one had to explain to people that 220 to 20 on a Friday afternoon wasn't really quite what it seemed.

I've been twice asked to go on a committee — the Finance Bill committee upstairs — where I think the demand is quite high: far more people want to get on it than do get on it. In both cases I wrote to the Chairman of Selection and also mentioned it to the whips.

The whips mainly decide, but I know that a minister in charge of a bill can go along to his whips and say, 'Well now, I'd like A, B and C on this committee.'

In one case, reported by a Conservative Member, he and a colleague, who along with two dozen other Conservatives had defied the whip on the second reading of a bill, actually went along to the Chief Whip to discuss with him how many rebels should serve on the Conservative side of the committee.

And we were pleased to get his agreement on the basic structure of the committee: that is, that there would be two people who had taken our view on it on second reading, two people out of four names we discussed.

The phrase 'other things being equal' was used a moment ago; but of course other things are not always equal. The whips, although they will generally want to accede to Members' wishes, also want to prevent their side of a committee from containing too many potential rebels. The Left were sure that during the period of the Labour Government the whips had at first deliberately excluded them from all standing committees dealing with prices and incomes legislation and had then included one or two only under pressure.

A deliberate effort was made, and at one stage we had to get a meeting with the leadership of the party. We were virtually excluded. Two were eventually allowed on, but never more than two. In other words, they carefully calculated how many from our section they could include without their losing the bill.

Someone sitting across the table interjected:

It would be a bit unreasonable to expect the Government whips to put people on a committee in such a way as to ensure that a Government bill was defeated. I mean to say ...

Not only do the whips want to avoid putting rebels on if they can avoid it: they also operate somewhat different criteria depending on whether they are in government or in opposition. What these criteria are can be inferred from the somewhat sardonic comments of a Conservative backbencher who, on one standing committee, had had a rather bad experience.

If you want to have influence, you adopt — or at least you should adopt — a different technique depending on which side you're on. Now someone mentioned ——[another Tory MP] a moment ago; let me just cite him as an example. On the first bill upstairs in 1971, ——insisted on keeping some of us up half the night, two nights running, talking about something or other. Now that was the end for many of us as far as —— was concerned. We had been kept out of our beds for four hours by the so-and-so. A couple of five-minute speeches and two equally short replies would have kept us out of bed for maybe twenty minutes and would have been far more influential.
   Now, against that, I would have thought that, if you're on the opposition side, then you talk — and you can even earn respect with the government side by keeping them out of bed for a long time, by adopting obstructionist techniques, and so on. So the point I want to make is that on standing committees — and on bills in the chamber too — there are different techniques. In government, brevity, a few points made, some punch, and that's the end: sit down and shut up. In opposition, you admire the man who can go on and on talking about sweet damn all.

A Labour ex-minister, however, was mildly indignant at the suggestion that delay is all that matters.

When I was leading for the Opposition on a bill, I was consulted by the whips as to who should go on that committee, and I was asked how I felt about A, B and C on our side and about X, Y and Z. And I'm bound to say I didn't want people just to get up and make very long and very tedious speeches to infuriate the Government. I think the fact that one goes through a bill line by line, almost word by word, is in itself a justification for the committee system — because, not only does an Opposition show up defects in a bill which, because they are purely practical ones within the purpose of the bill, the

Government are likely to accept, but occasionally the Opposition can actually persuade the Government to change its mind. Infuriating the Government is not the object of the exercise.

But, if infuriating the Government is not always the object of the exercise, causing obstruction frequently is. Another former Labour minister was not a little proud of his part in holding up week after week a not wholly insignificant Government bill.

It has been suggested that I hold, for this century at any rate, the record for delay of a bill. That was a two-page bill to bring back fee-paying in Scottish schools. It went on for five months. I had to keep it going till the May local government elections, and I had exactly two pages to work on. And on those two pages only something like ten to twenty lines were amendable. I had to put down hundreds of amendments on those two pages; it was an intellectual exercise: getting amendments down that were in order; every two hours they put the motion for closure of the debate on that clause; they voted; we got beaten; on we went. But I had to keep it going till May, and I did. Now this had little to do with trying to amend the bill: it was basically a delaying operation.

One of his colleagues sought to justify the proceeding.

One thing people around this table – and a lot of other people – tend to forget is that almost the only weapon an Opposition has is time. Almost the only thing one can do is to deny the Government a certain amount of time. If you can persuade the Government, fine. If not, time is all you have.

Perhaps the severest limitation on the work of standing committees is the one mentioned at the beginning of this chapter: their inability to examine experts and cross-examine ministers and civil servants – in other words, to conduct investigations. But of course there is nothing to stop individual members of a standing committee, in their own time and on their own initiative, from carrying out their own investigations. In fact, however, they seldom do, and it was a rare instance of such private enterprise – perhaps not unrelated to the nature of the subject – that was described by a senior Tory.

It was on the Betting and Gaming Bill of a year or two back. Some of us looked at it and decided it didn't seem quite right; and so we took to the gaming clubs. Four of us had three or four hilarious nights, starting with a very good establishment in Curzon Street, going on to the Playboy, then going on to the sort of middle grade, and finishing up in some very odd places – with a police escort, provided by the Home Secretary, who gave us his blessing. As a result, we really did form the conclusion that the whole basis in the Bill of the attempt to control betting and gaming establishments was a nonsense. And the committee produced a bill that was totally different from anything the Home Office – who I don't suppose go to the Playboy much – had conceived of. And, what is more, after our tour we found we'd turned in a profit of £45! [*Laughter*].

This story is interesting largely because most MPs, if they heard it without having been told beforehand that it related to the work of a standing committee, would almost certainly assume that the four parliamentary gamesters were conducting their investigation as part of the work of an entirely different kind of body: a select committee. Select committees, as their name does not suggest, are committees concerned with keeping under review some designated area of policy or administration. The Public Accounts Committee, for example, is charged with ensuring that all public monies are spent as Parliament intended; the Expenditure Committee considers long-term trends in government spending and assesses the effectiveness of departmental administration; the Select Committee on Race Relations and Immigration has investigated such matters as employment opportunities for coloured school-leavers. Some select committees have enormously broad terms of reference; the Science and Technology Committee, to take an extreme case, is empowered in the most sweeping way 'to consider science and technology and to report'.

Some select committees are more permanent than others; each does its own work in its own way. But they all have certain common characteristics which distinguish them sharply from standing committees. Whereas standing committees debate specific pieces of legislation, select committees as a rule do not. Whereas standing committees are non-specialist, most select committees attract, and are meant to attract, Members interested in their particular subject. Whereas a standing committee simply debates a bill and, as a committee, never examines witnesses or conducts an investigation, a select committee is expected to do precisely both of these things. The product of a standing committee is a bill, amended or unamended; the product of a select committee is a report to the House.

There is another way in which select committees differ from standing committees, which is not inevitable and which is not written down in any formal rule but which none the less profoundly affects their work. Standing committees, at least on bills that are controversial between the parties, operate in a highly partisan manner: speeches are party speeches, and the whips are on. By contrast, it is generally agreed that select committees should be non-partisan. The general view is that they can make their most useful contribution in fields where there is little party-political disagreement or other political controversy and in which therefore Members can function not as Labour Members or Tory Members but simply as Members. Select committees would of course probably be restricted to these sorts of fields anyway, since a Government finding a select committee being used as an effective platform by the Opposition or by critics on its own back benches would probably simply use its majority to wind it up. Exactly this happened in the case of the Select Committee on Agriculture, which died a very sudden death in 1968 after it had dared, against the Government's wishes, to investigate the probable consequences for British agriculture of Britain's entry into the EEC.

Despite these limitations, or perhaps because of them, most Members at the dinners were enthusiastic about the select committee system. It had, they thought, a whole string of advantages.

You can get the minister and grill him – grill him in an all-party atmosphere. If he doesn't answer, you can keep going at him until you get the answer. A minister can't be evasive in a select committee the way he can in the House. Probing shows up the gaps.

I think select committees have the great advantage that the civil service are kept on their toes. Civil servants know weeks beforehand if they are going to be expected to appear before a committee, and it does them good to have to bone up on the answers to all the questions they might conceivably get asked.

At least one Conservative liked the system mainly because it is good for Members themselves: it makes them do their homework.

The point is that anyone can sit in the chamber and, having done very little homework, get up and make a speech. But you can't get away with that in a select committee. You're exploring the minds of civil servants and ministers and experts of all kinds, and, if you haven't prepared yourself thoroughly, everybody soon knows it.

Except when they are actually writing their reports, most select committees meet in public, with the bulk of their evidence published afterwards. This taking of evidence in public some Members regard as almost more important than the subsequent reports. One Member reported that a select committee chairman had said to him:

'You should see that you sit at a time suitable to the press. Sit in the mornings at 10.30; then the press will come. Begin to consider that the function of the committee is not so much to report to the House – you do that automatically anyway – as to have a discussion in the open, rather the way the Americans do.'

By the same token, because they seldom go over the same ground as the House of Commons as a whole, select committees increase the number of subjects that Members can consider and also make it possible for second-rank subjects to be looked at seriously.

On an issue of absolutely first-rate importance, like Europe, anything that is worth saying at all is going to come out in the course of the endless debates in the House. It's on the issues of less than outstanding importance where I think Parliament is at its very worst. You can go for months and even years without getting any sensible discussion at all.

Take overseas aid, which two or three of us are interested in. In the Congress of the United States there are major discussions on the Foreign Aid Bill every year. Here you get the odd day, and a badly attended day, on the floor of the House every other year. But this is a subject which is ideal, in fact, for the select committee procedure: you can go into detail, you can make recommendations.

The attractions of select committee work are obvious: the chance to confront ministers and civil servants, the opportunity to become master of one's subject. A lot of Members also relish the chance to gang up on the Government; the select committee system is almost unique in the House of Commons in pitting the legislature against the executive in a non-partisan – one might almost say a trans-partisan – way. The system, as a Conservative put it, causes MPs on both sides to take up 'a natural stance of opposition'. It can also generate a certain excitement.

What is interesting is that nothing ever goes the way you expect it to. You have a series of questions prepared beforehand, which you study. They may cover several pages. But then, it's like a law case: suddenly you begin to penetrate in a way that you didn't expect and to reveal a weakness.

The fact remains, however, that it is often hard to get Members to serve on select committees. The work, although it has its moments, is demanding and laborious, seldom attracts publicity and tends to deal with the less momentous issues. Perhaps most important, select committees do not, except very occasionally, take decisions. They discuss, they investigate, they report; but, unlike standing committees, they do not decide. They have indeed a faintly academic air about them. This quality attracts some MPs; but it undoubtedly repels others.

How much influence select committees have is disputed. Some Members maintained that, although select committees seldom make a direct impact, their views are taken seriously by civil servants and others knowledgeable about particular subjects.

A number of our recommendations have now been accepted. And I'm sure that the evidence we took – although it was read by nobody else – was read within the Ministry and had an effect on the discussions within the Ministry.

I think some committees virtually produce bills. The Select Committee on the Nationalised Industries may not often have its reports debated in the House, but very often they're the basis for the next bill for the gas industry or the coal industry or the reorganisation of the Post Office. My guess is that the next bill on the television companies will come out of that last select committee report on the IBA [Independent Broadcasting Authority].

What is clear is that select committees owe what influence they have, not to their power or even to their ability to command publicity, which at present is minimal, but simply to the weight of the arguments and evidence they bring to bear.

Most of our MPs were prepared to put in a good word for the present select committee system. They did not assign select committees a very important role under present circumstances, but they clearly thought them on balance to be a good thing. The same was not true with regard to standing committees. On the contrary: not one of the Members at either of the dinners where committees were discussed was prepared to commend the present system of standing committees or even to defend it — except on the ground that it is hard to think of a workable alternative. One Labour Member, indeed, thought the whole subject too ludicrous to be worth talking about at all.

Could I say that it distresses me that we have spent so much time tonight discussing something of so little importance? The Government makes up its mind, the Government introduces a bill, the Government sends it to a committee, the committee goes through the motions. And that is all there is to it: going through the motions. Let us not be in any doubt.

The standing committee system was criticised on four grounds. Firstly, because the standing committee stage of so many bills is conducted in a highly partisan way, Opposition Members have fewer chances than they should have of carrying amendments. Secondly, for the same reason, and also because the Government is usually anxious to get its bills through as quickly as possible, Government Members, although they may stand a better chance than Opposition Members of having their amendments accepted, are disinclined to press them. Thirdly, standing committees cannot cross-examine ministers and have no access to the civil servants who prepare bills; they cannot call in independent witnesses. Fourthly, for all of these reasons, standing committees can be a great waste of time.

These sentiments were expressed by Members of both parties and of all age groups. They were certainly not confined to the Opposition or to the rebellious young. The following quotations catch their spirit.

How satisfied are the people sitting around this table that, given a Government bill, the standing committee system is the best way of dealing with it?

Totally dissatisfied as far as I'm concerned. In government it's best to keep quiet and get on with your correspondence. In opposition you're expected to take as much time as possible. I don't think either role is particularly rewarding.

The present system isn't in any way designed to improve legislation on which there is a deep division of opinion on party lines.

The Opposition talk as much as they can and prolong the thing; the Government have a strong incentive to wrap up and shut up. Consequently, this makes one as a Government backbencher very reluctant, unless one feels very strongly about something, to try and change anything.

The present temptation is for a Government to staff its side with people who don't give a damn about the bill – just let it get through.

The Housing Finance Bill went on for 257 hours, and in all that time we didn't learn anything and we didn't contribute anything. I should think every member of that committee, because it went on so long, spent more time outside the committee room than inside it: dictating letters to their secretary, and so on.

On so many bills you just go over the same ground again and again and again.

Several Members, although critical of the present system, were, in the words of one of them, 'blowed' if they could think of anything better. But most of them had positive suggestions to make, and two possible avenues of change were opened up. One – the less drastic of the two – was that the Opposition, and in particular Opposition front-bench spokesmen, should be provided with some substantial portion of the briefing material available to the Government. One Labour Member argued this case in some detail.

When I was an Opposition spokesman, the one thing I didn't have was any expertise on my side equivalent to the civil service expertise on the other – even in such basics as looking through a bill and saying, 'Well now, the effect of Clause 1 is X, Y and Z, but of course, if you amended it in a certain particular, then you'd have to watch the effect the amendment would have on this or that other piece of legislation.' Just sheer technical advice on points of this kind.

More than that. Anybody who's been in government and seen a bill going through knows that the civil service produces for the minister in charge, first the bill itself, then headings on the bill, then

comments on the bill, then a vast chunk of information telling him
precisely what Clause 1 means and what it's going to do and how it
affects X, Y and Z, and the minister should be careful because it
might affect A, B and C as well — vast quantities of stuff. Now I
don't see any real reason why this basic, almost technical information
shouldn't be available to the other side of the committee as well. I
had one little bill in Government and for the committee stage I had a
great pile of paper in front of me. Frankly, from the Government
point of view, if it had been available to the rest of the House, it
would on the whole have assisted the passage of the bill. It certainly
would have saved me having to make a lot of unnecessary explanations.

Despite this last point, the briefing of Opposition spokesmen
would undoubtedly to some extent strengthen the Opposition.
None the less, the change, although possibly desirable, would
in no way be fundamental.

The other possibility discussed at the dinners could, if
adopted, have more drastic repercussions. This was that the
standing committee system should somehow be 'married' to
the select committee system. The idea is not a new one, but
the amount of support it got from MPs of both parties was
surprising. The marriage could take a variety of forms: the
creation of a Select Committee on Bills; alternatively the referring of all bills to a network of select committees modelled
on the present ones but extending over the entire range of
government activity. Either way, the aim would be to ensure
that the committees dealing with legislation had the power to
cross-examine ministers, civil servants and other witnesses.
Several Members also hoped that the new committee or committees would see the end of the extreme partisanship that
characterises standing committees in their present form.

As one would expect, some of the reasons Members gave for
wanting to effect the marriage were very similar to their reasons for liking select committees as they are now.

The minister can get away with murder in standing committee or in
the House. You make a speech; he simply doesn't answer your point,
and since you can't cross-examine him you have no comeback.

I've recently been on a standing committee and also on a select committee dealing with the same thing, and I can't begin to describe the
different tempo and atmosphere and way of doing business between

them even though roughly the same chaps were involved. The select committee method is much better.

If we could have bills considered by the interested people on both sides, it would be worth while. On the one side it would weaken the Government's position, but it would equally weaken the Opposition's because the Government might well pick up support from the Opposition from specialised, interested people.

In addition, two other arguments were advanced, both relating specifically to legislation. A Conservative hoped that the creation of a Select Committee on Bills would somehow make it possible to sharpen the separation between the debates on the principles of a bill and the examination of its details. His complaint was that, under the present system, the standing committee, instead of getting down to detail, often repeats endlessly arguments that have already been made on second reading.

Let's take an example. Take Barbara Castle's proposal in the Road Safety Bill to make the breathalyser a random spot-check instead of the one we've got now. That was a major matter of principle, which I think could have been disposed of early on instead of dragging on and on as it did and getting entangled with the details. A Select Committee on Bills would certainly be a time-saver.

A Labour Member thought that, if bills were dealt with in a select committee style, groups outside Parliament could be brought directly into the legislative process.

When you come to legislation with a real political content – where it might be possible to convince society at large that a proposal would be harmful, but where it's not possible to convince the Government – the present standing committees can never achieve anything. But just possibly, if you had a select committee approach, you might make contact with pressure groups in that particular field and break through the Government's ideology and force it to change its mind.

Our discussion of a major recasting of the committee system – like our discussion in the last chapter on the influence of backbenchers on major Government policies – was inconclusive. In particular, no very detailed consideration was given to what the consequences of such a major recasting might be. On the one hand, as at least one Member recognised, the change might have only limited consequences if the

Government succeeded in introducing into the new committees a party discipline as rigorous as in the present standing committees. On the other, if the new system did lead to a greater disposition to consider Government bills 'on their merits' and if it did result in a weakening of party discipline, then a major shift in the balance of power between Government and backbenchers would have taken place and the British system would have come to resemble the American or, more probably, the West German. The consequences of a major recasting would be exceedingly hard to predict. They would almost certainly be far-reaching.

9 MPs on their Work

Readers of this book will be aware by now – the Members of
Parliament who took part in the dinners certainly were – of all
the important things we did not have time to discuss. We
devoted almost no time to the MP's relationship with television and the press (this despite Granada's sponsorship of the
dinners); we did not have a proper discussion of the Opposition's functions in the House or of the tactical alternatives
open to it; we said hardly anything about private members'
legislation; we did not consider what the consequences for
Parliament will be of Britain's entry into the European Community; the House of Lords in twenty hours of conversation
was mentioned exactly once. Even the discussions we did have
were never as thorough as we would have liked. The portrait
of parliamentary life presented in these pages is therefore, although we hope broadly accurate, by no means complete.

But there were two additional subjects which it did seem
worth devoting some time to. One was what our MPs felt to
be the most rewarding – and the most frustrating – aspects of
life in the House. The other was their assessment of the role of
Parliament in the government of modern Britain. The fact that
the dinners were held at all implies a certain view about the
importance of the House of Commons in our political system.
But is the House important? Does it matter? These questions
constituted the central theme of all our discussions. Most of
our MPs turned out to have thought about them a good deal.

What Members like and dislike about the House is of considerable intrinsic interest; one is invited to consider how the
occupation of politics differs from other occupations, and to
speculate about why people go into politics in the first place.
Members' likes and dislikes also yield a number of pointers to
the forms that pressure might take for changes in the way the
House operates. Our discussion could hardly have been more
diverse: the things that some Members liked most about the
House were precisely the things that others liked least.

If there was one thing almost all of them enjoyed, it was the sense of being at the centre of things: of being where the action is — though it was striking how many of them, in conveying this sense, used the language less of the active participant than of the spectator.

It's the endless fascination of having a front row in the stalls at the most interesting of all theatrical performances. One does feel, or I feel, that one is pretty close to the centre of the stage of the major affairs of the country.

You're at the centre of what's going on — yet, paradoxically, you have to buy a paper at the end of the week to find out what's been happening in the world.

The opportunity I like most is of course simply being near the place, the House of Commons, where power resides and where people are making decisions — and you're taking part in those decisions.

A Conservative summed it up.

We're very lucky to be engaged in what F.S. Oliver called 'the endless adventure of governing men'. It really is a great adventure, and it undoubtedly repays all the chores.

Several of those who had had long spells in other occupations agreed that being an MP has much more to offer.

The chores are all there, the frustrations are all there, but the opportunities are all there too. And, because it offers these opportunities, I find it a wider, more exciting thing than any other profession I've been in.

Another Member also emphasised Parliament's almost unlimited range.

It's a far, far more broadening experience than anything else. One realises this when one goes back to see one's colleagues in industry, those who are engaged full time in industry: one does realise just how blinkered their life is.

The thing that Members complained most about was, as one of them put it, 'the drudgery' of constituency work.

An awful lot of constituency stuff really belongs to local councillors, but it comes our way. We really ought to have the strength to say, 'I'm sorry, this goes to your local councillor or your county councillor.' This would reduce our correspondence and casework, I would say, by 60 per cent.

Another Member was much more vehement.

It does seem to me tragic that we've reached this position – it's our own fault – where we've conned the public into believing that we can tell the local councils what to do. All my constituents believe it. And I find I'm wasting more and more time; it's not what I was elected to do. I find it terribly frustrating and annoying. You advertise a surgery. Everybody comes along to see you. Once I've been at this, let's say, from 10.30 till 1.30 and again from 2.30 till 5.30 I find it terribly difficult to keep my temper with anyone, no matter how well I started off at the beginning of the day. It's all the same thing: housing and everything, drains, dustbins, you name it.

Many complained; but for some constituency work was the very thing they enjoyed most.

I like to be able to say that I can deal with matters: that I can sort out the poor sods who need to be sorted out, and that includes very often the Gas Board, the Electricity Board, Health and Social Security, and so on.

I get a lot of satisfaction out of just being able now and then to strengthen the position of my own constituency against the faceless bureaucracies – whether it's in nationalised industries or government departments – to give them that little bit of backing they need.

Even one of those who complained most vociferously about the drudgery felt constrained to add:

I do have to admit that there is, very occasionally, a moment of reward, when you succeed perhaps in a very small thing – to do with a pensioner or something like that. Those moments really make up for an awful lot of the minuses.

The life of politics is, among other things, a life of conflict. Personal rivalries are probably no more numerous in politics than in other lines of business and, except possibly at the very top, they are probably no more intense. But such rivalries do exist, and in politics they are compounded by all sorts of other conflicts: between parties, factions and contending points of view. In some of this conflict, especially between the parties, there is undoubtedly an element of charade; but anyone who has been in politics or observed it at first hand cannot doubt that much of it – over industrial relations and race relations, for example – is real. How much someone enjoys parliamentary life will depend to some extent on whether he or she can be indifferent to this element of conflict, or alternatively positively enjoy it.

It was interesting that few Members at the dinners referred explicitly to any dislike of conflict, or indeed expressed any personal animosity towards other MPs. On the contrary, a number made a point of emphasising the comradeship of politics.

I like being able to say that my friends include people in my party whose views are known to differ completely from mine.

Without being sentimental.... [*You are being!*]..... one of the most delightful things is the friendship amongst people on all sides of the House. You think somebody's the most frightful creep, and then you get to know him and in fact you find he's a terribly nice person.

A Labour Member took pleasure in the contrast between what the newspapers say goes on and what actually does.

The best thing in politics is the comradeship: the fact that one can sit in the tea room, when the London evening papers are talking about uproar in the Labour Party — 'the knives are out, they're cutting each other's throats' — and in actual fact we're all sitting in the tea room buying each other cups of tea.

Only one Member, also on the Labour side, confessed that all this talk of friendship struck him as completely phoney — or at least as not the way things felt to him.

We've been turned on with the delights of Parliament: friendships and the tea room. You remember Oscar Wilde saying, 'Who can read about the death of Little Nell without bursting into laughter?' I feel exactly the same about this description. I loathe the House of Commons, loathe it. I can't sit here without leaning my back against the chair in case somebody puts a knife in it. I've never known such backbiting and personal nastiness in all my life. My Nonconformist soul squirms. I hate it.

It is only right to add that at this point most of this Member's colleagues looked a trifle amazed. 'But I couldn't fall out with you', one of them kept saying, 'I just couldn't.'

Whether one loves or loathes the House is clearly largely a matter of temperament and personal experience. Similarly, one's view about whether or not the House is a satisfying place in which to work is likely to be partly determined by whether or not one believes that Parliament actually exercises real influence on government. Someone who believes, or persuades himself, that Parliament does have real influence is, other things being equal, likelier to be happy in the House than someone who does not. Certainly the MPs at the dinners who seemed least contented in Parliament were those who believe either that they themselves have no influence as individuals or that the House as a whole has very little. One such was the Labour Member quoted in an earlier chapter who thought that debates in the chamber were a 'farce'. Another was a Conservative, who remarked with considerable vehemence:

We get a lot of Members not bothering to take part on the floor or in committee because they think it's just not worth while: because there's nothing we can say or do which will alter the Government's or the minister's mind. And this is frustrating. We are not dealing with 630 unintelligent people, and the British Government have got to wake up to this fact. There is a measure of frustration which is unbelievable in the House of Commons today. People are very fed up indeed, and I for one am very fed up: very fed up with this misapplication of people, who know a subject but know they can't do anything about it unless they're prepared to go to the wall.

The majority of our Members, by contrast, even if they did not think the House has enough influence, were still buoyed up by the sense that some of what they say matters some of the time – or might do in the future. Asked what he enjoyed most about being an MP, a younger Conservative replied:

I think first of all just being a representative under our system, and all the things that go with that: the people, the groups who come and see you and feel that you can be of some influence and that you can exert that influence in Parliament. Then the fact that about once a year one is able to influence some decision that is being made by Government. And, thirdly, I suppose still the hope that one day one might be allowed to play with the big boys. If one is really honest, at the moment one plays the little games; but there's always the hope dangled in front of one that some day in government one might be able to influence the big decisions.

A Labour Member, also young, who insisted he was speaking about his party and not just about himself, went further.

What is enjoyable about politics? Power and the exercise of power, which I find absolutely delightful. If I thought for one moment I was going to spend forty years in the House of Commons and never exercise power again, I would find it an absolutely dreadful and appalling and arid prospect. What do I find most disagreeable about politics? Being deprived of power, in the sense that one can't do anything. It's as basic and simple as that.

Only a few Labour Members, however, drew the distinction between government and opposition quite so sharply.

Frustration was the main single source of dissatisfaction among our Members; but there were certainly other things that many of them disliked.

The inroads Parliament makes on one's personal life: the sheer demands of time, so that one will spend most of the time down here, at weekends in the constituency. It's a cost we all know about — that we're prepared to pay — but nevertheless it's a hell of a cost.
Not just you but the family.
Exactly.

The inability to plan one's life ahead for large parts of the year. One cannot say I will be somewhere a month ahead because something will blow up two days before and you will have to cancel the whole thing. One is not one's own master as far as one's life is concerned.

The nut cases who ring me up at midnight.

Quite simply the long hours. I hate staying up night after night till midnight and after. What irritates me most is the staying up till 2 o'clock in the morning to see that the Government can move the closure or has a quorum — especially when everybody else seems to have gone off.

The fact that neither I nor my opposite number is ever allowed to forget for one moment that we are party politicians, and that his job is simply either to oppose legislation or support it depending which side he's on. I remember on one bill one of my colleagues saying, 'Oh well, we can keep this going for ten committee meetings.' But why keep it going for ten if it's not worth more than five?

But, apart from all this, there is the question of what kind of job it is supposed to be. As one Conservative pointed out, the strange hours and the lack of secretarial help are holdovers from a time when being a Member of Parliament was something one did in one's spare time.

The final thing I find maddening about the present system is the conflict that we've not yet resolved as to whether being a Member of Parliament in Britain is an amateur or a professional occupation. I can see it being played both ways, and I would be quite happy to do it either way; but at the moment it seems to me we're screwed between the two. In effect, the work is there for being a full-time Member provided he has the right facilities and is aided to do it. It's ridiculous doing filing and all that sort of nonsense when one could be spending one's time much better being really well informed on one or two subjects and exerting an influence. On the other hand, there is still the strong feeling that this is a game for gentlemen who have other things to do, and that what you should really do is earn your money and pay your way, and then drift over to the House and, you know, deliver your opinions and so on. There's a great conflict here that we haven't sorted out, and I find it very frustrating.

It was evident from what a large number of Members said that the more seriously one takes one's job as an MP, the more infuriating the lack of facilities is.

All of our MPs, even the ones – the majority – who were reasonably contented in Parliament, disliked something or other about life in the House; and most of them had proposals for change, ranging from (again) the provision of more secretarial help through the restructuring of the committee system to the holding of votes in the House on one day of the week. Yet it would be misleading to give the impression that everyone at the dinners believed change to be terribly important. Two at least did not. Both were Conservatives, but it is hard to believe that their views are to be found only on the Tory side. They were asked, if each were allowed to introduce a single reform into the House of Commons, what it would be.

I can answer the question, but the main thing is that I'm really pretty happy with the way I work: with the conditions in which I work. I suppose it's like Rex Harrison in *My Fair Lady:* I've grown accustomed to her face. I'm not one for an office in a new building: I'm one for a small desk to put your case on and then go to the chamber or the committee room or the tea room and be in the House of Commons. I'm happy.

The other argued – not at all complacently but in the belief that all is not well in Britain – that there is something to be said for letting well enough alone.

If there is one criticism of ourselves that we all might make in response to this question, it's that the pressures of life are such that none of us is able to read as much as we should like. That I'm absolutely sure of, though I say it rather pompously having just succeeded in getting through de Tocqueville's *Democracy in America* for the second time. And I do recall a rather good sentence which I think is not inappropriate. In his chapter on the press, he says something to the effect that we are all in favour of a free press — if only we could get rid of the blemishes. You know, if we could just remove the excesses and so on, then we would all be in favour of it.

What he meant, of course, is that this is the sort of delusion that societies, when they are slightly sick in mind and not really thinking straight, suffer from. And I believe that that really has some application for free parliaments as well. I think we all of us get into a mood when we feel that, if only we can correct this, and this, and this, and that, we can make a running go of it. And there are any number of people outside Parliament who would encourage us in this. People would want endless reform to make the thing work, and I think the time comes when you have to ask yourself, 'Well, do we believe in the institution as it is, representing the free democracy?' And, if we do, where do we stick our heels in and say, 'All right, we agree in detail — we'll alter this and alter that — but if you aren't very careful we'll all lose completely something that has been formulated over six hundred years'?

Some Members are happy in Parliament because they think the House of Commons matters; others are relatively unhappy because they think it does not. But to know that a particular MP thinks the one or the other is not to know on what he bases his judgement. How do MPs assess the influence of the House? The answer began to emerge in the course of our earlier discussion, in Chapter 7, on the impact of debates and questions in the chamber; but we returned to it later in rather more general terms. This part of the discussion also took place mainly at one of the Labour dinners.

The remark that sparked off the discussion was this:

You ask, when we speak in Parliament, who are we talking to. But what is the significance of this anyhow? You should start by asking what is the significance of the system of democracy in this country as a whole. It's extraordinary: the thing that mystifies me most is that anyone takes any notice at all of this miscellaneous collection of people who've been elected by their constituents. What's it matter who you're talking to? If you're reported in the local press, what's the significance of that? If you're reported in *The Times,* what's the significance of that? There are certain powerful bodies in this country that determine the way this country goes. The House of Commons is not one of them.

Someone else, a little startled, asked whether this MP was simply saying that a lot that goes on in the House of Commons does not make much difference.

Well, I'm saying that, but I'm really saying something rather more than that: that the whole system has lost meaning. Why it goes on working is one of the great mysteries of British politics. It's completely lost meaning and the real question is how you inject some meaning into it.

'Television cameras', someone interjected hopefully.

No, not by television cameras. Politics is about power, and running a country is about the way in which you get those who happen in the country to have power to agree on some way of living together and doing things. Now the House of Commons just hasn't got these sorts of people in it – the people with real power of their own.

By this time there was evident dismay around the table, and several people wanted to know whether the Member in question did not perhaps mean something more limited. Perhaps he was merely saying that the House was not as effective a check on the executive as it should be. But he was not to be put off.

The House of Commons is completely remote from running the country. What misleads people is this. Governments in this country do have some power – some – and Governments are made up of a group of people who have got there because they are members of the House of Commons. Momentarily, when you're in government, you're in a special position; you suddenly happen to have power. And the Government you are in was formed from the House of Commons. But the real question is how you use the power you get by being in government in relation to all the other people who have power in the country. And to this question, this process, the House of Commons is virtually totally irrelevant.

He added:

The point I'm arguing is where power lies in this country: the amount of power that is created out of the democratic process, and how it is used, as compared with the other sorts of power that exist in the country. The fact of the matter is that the power created out of the democratic process is now smaller than it has been for a very long time.

Several Members looked impressed by this argument, but no one was quite prepared to accept all of it and several disagreed vehemently.

No, I can't accept that. We are in the middle of a parliament in which the elected Government first did a number of things — quite rightly according to its manifesto — and then in the space of two years, with breath-taking suddenness, has totally reversed its policy from one thing to another. Now I cannot believe that during this time, when ministers were discussing things behind the scenes, that they discounted the reaction of the House of Commons and the reaction of the country, which is after all part of 'the democratic process'. The other thing is that the House of Commons is more difficult for a Government than the country because, when somebody makes a point in the House, the Government often has to recognise that he really does have a point. I don't take a despairing attitude. Maybe the House of Commons doesn't have *real* power, but the important thing is that Governments believe it has power and are willing to credit the House of Commons with an ability to influence events — not overwhelmingly, but to a large extent.

Another Member returned again to the Labour Government's defeat on industrial relations, and another reiterated the point that a Government which loses the confidence of its own backbenchers typically finds that it can no longer do some of the things it wants to do.

Up to this point, the argument lay between those who contended that the House of Commons has no real influence as compared with other forces in the country (though only the one Member took quite this extreme view) and those who maintained that it does have real influence, and that the House — by itself, by what is said and done in it — can force Governments to change course. One or two Members, however, took a somewhat different view: that the House can make an impact on a Government, but only provided Members in the House are in some sense the spokesmen of real political forces outside. The Members need not merely reflect the opinions of such forces, but they do have to stand in some sort of relationship to them. This view was put most vigorously by a former Minister.

I think what is missing here is the other element. Parliament is not important in itself, except in relation to the political structures and movements outside. If you take the example we keep coming back to — the defeat of *In Place of Strife* — it was not only because it ran afoul of the Parliamentary Labour Party; it was also because the trade unions said, 'It's not on.' And, with the best will in the world, a Government cannot govern if the people suddenly say, 'It's not on.' One way or another it'll be stopped.

Now on this one you had the combination of the trade unions expressing their views and the Commons — the governing party — pressing ministers, and it eventually percolated through to the Cabinet that it wasn't on. In other words, the parliamentary debate, the parliamentary scene, is only the apex of the whole changing political movement. The things we do here matter to the extent that they tap, or reflect, or move forward these movements in the country as a whole. And what alarms me at the present time in Parliament is that so much of the discussion that goes on is divorced from the truths and realities that exist outside. Once we realise that the House of Commons only becomes important when it reflects or strengthens outside movements, then parliamentary debate and so on could become more important because it would reflect such a link-up. I think Governments can be changed by what happens in the House of Commons but only because — and when — the House of Commons is not isolated. Once we've understood this point, we both minimise the importance of Parliament if seen in isolation and realise that it's more important if we see it in relation to things going on outside.

'Here', he concluded, 'endeth my lesson.'

If some Members believe that the House of Commons has almost no influence and many more believe that, although it has some, it ought to have more, what do they think should be done? Several answers to this question have already been given. The Member just quoted wished to see the forging of new kinds of links between the House and other political forces in the country. Quite a few MPs on both sides thought that a strengthened House of Commons was one of the many advantages to be gained from overhauling the committee system. Still others wanted extra facilities not merely to ease their own burdens of work but to make both themselves and the House more effective. But it was perhaps significant that, on top of all this, a considerable number of Members, both Labour and Conservative, were ready to insist that the present degree of party discipline in the House of Commons is much too great and should, or will, no longer be tolerated. In the past, this view has been confined largely to the left wing of the Labour Party and to other scattered individualists. To judge from our dinners, it is now probably fairly widespread on the back benches on both sides.

The Labour Member quoted a few moments ago was arguing that the House of Commons would become important again only when the men of power in the country were again members of it. One of his colleagues took the general point but thought the inference to be drawn was quite the reverse.

What ———— was saying was: get the power base in the country properly represented in the House and the House will have power. It's absolutely true, but I think he's upending it. The answer is: let those who happen by the irrelevant procedures of today to have got into the House of Commons actually take decisions – wise, stupid, wicked or whatever – and then the power base in the country will have to come into the House of Commons. Create a situation in which Members of Parliament take decisions and then people will wish to achieve this office.

And this Member was equally clear about how in fact the House could come to take decisions again.

The secret of the whole operation is: are Members prepared to be persuaded? Somebody not known for his outstanding commentaries on parliamentary life said to me in the tea room the other day something I've written down in my diary and been passing around. His remark was that any Member of Parliament in this place who thinks he can convince a colleague of anything by persuasion has got another think coming. And that's what is wrong with the House of Commons: we are not prepared to be persuaded. And why not? Because we are not able to detach any significant number of people from the other side to vote for us; nor can they talk us into voting with them. And this wholly weakens the position of the House: we, as a result, do not take the decisions.

These views did not meet with universal assent.

What in fact do you mean? It's a lot of generalisation. Do you want to alter policy? What do you mean?
I mean that, when the executive, the Government, brings proposals to the House, it is the House that finally decides.
You just mean your view ought to prevail.
No, the view of the majority of the House ought to prevail. We

would then have not only a Parliament that looked as if it was deserving of its keep but also, in fact, better government.

This Member concluded:

What's wrong with British parliamentary democracy is, quite simply, that people are not prepared to vote against their own Government — perhaps on rare occasions, when they think it really matters a great deal, but not otherwise. On everything else, they may vote against their Government on an odd occasion, when they know the Government won't be defeated, perhaps sometimes in committee, but never if they think it'll hurt. Because people kid themselves into believing that, even on less important things, adverse votes will bring the Government down they don't vote against the Government. The result is that, in a whole myriad of decisions which are of secondary and third-rank importance, you get bad decisions — and, what is important, bad decisions taken with a majority of the House or the committee or whatever knowing they are bad decisions. That's what's wrong with the system.

Another Labour Member — someone from an entirely different part of the party's ideological spectrum — thought that the best way of encouraging Government backbenchers to rebel would be to have parliaments with fixed terms.

The function of the back-bench MP is very different from the function of those in the Government. This is what we have got to get understood. And this means starting with fundamentals. We must have a fixed period for parliaments, so that, if the Government is defeated, there is none of this nonsense about its going to the country. The only way in which the back-bench MP becomes really effective is when he is not faced continuously with this business of the Government or the Prime Minister saying, 'I will be compelled to go to the country if you persist in this business of objecting to this, that and the other.'

Few of his colleagues were prepared to accept this particular idea (though one did, enthusiastically); but the thought that it might be a good idea if Government backbenchers rebelled more often undoubtedly fell on less stony ground that it would have done in (say) the 1950s.

The Conservatives indicated their views not so much by what they said as by what they did: five of the nine attending the dinners had either abstained or voted against the Government in important divisions since the Conservatives were returned in 1970, and a sixth had been a persistent rebel in opposition. And one Tory did maintain stoutly at the dinners that the whole business of party discipline needs to be re-thought.

If the Government will not seek to persuade before it brings in legislation, and this means a consultative approach to its supporters, then it's going to have to face frustration more and more, because I suspect that Members of Parliament coming into the House now are a little less anxious just to be sheep following the shepherd, and are asking much more the question, 'Why should I support this? No-body's talked to me about it. It doesn't seem awfully good to me.' And I believe that reluctance is going to make itself felt. I would just quote a shadow minister on the other side – somebody I respect very much – who said to me recently, 'We've got to break the power of the whips. Governments must be prepared to be beaten and not mind too much, and realise this is the best way to improve democracy.'

Several of his colleagues claimed that more consultation went on than he seemed to realise, but it is perhaps significant that none of them seemed to want to challenge his central point directly.

The Granada dinners, through no one's fault, came to an end too quickly. A number of important subjects were, as we have said, passed over completely; and with more time we could have considered in much more detail the broad questions discussed in this chapter of Parliament's role in the British system of government and of how that role might change in the next few years.

Moreover, there was one other subject raised at the dinners – perhaps more important than any of these – that we did not have time to go into in detail: the question, not of Parliament's role within our system of government, but of our system of government's role within the broader society. It was the view of one of our Members that the capacity of Governments of either party to determine the broad course of our economic and social development has declined sharply over the past few years: that 'government in this country has lost significant power'.

I am deeply worried about the power of the Government – of any Government. It seems to me that the thing that's changed in society is that, whereas it once mattered what the Government of the day decided, now it matters a great deal less.

Take, he said, the rate of inflation as a measure of this.

One knows, for example, that in Latin America Governments, whether they're right-wing or left-wing or of no wing at all, whether they're Allende or Castro or somebody on the right, are completely without significance to what happens in the society unless they can really do something about the rate of inflation. And none of them can. Now we have in this country a roaring inflation: we have a rate of inflation which seems to me to mean that government is no longer as significant – anything like as significant – as it once was. If I or some other Member of Parliament influences a minister on some minor bill or other, that's fine: it gives us a certain amount of satisfaction and will be important to perhaps twenty thousand people in this country.

'But', he insisted, 'it won't be important to the country as a whole. And that's the worrying thing.'

We did not pursue this subject partly because we did not have the time but partly because this is clearly not a subject for Members of Parliament alone. It is a subject for MPs, to be sure, but also for economists, sociologists, political scientists and businessmen, and for all those with a practical or academic knowledge of other countries. The future of the environment is a fashionable subject at the moment – rightly so. Perhaps the future of government ought to be too.

Index